It Doesn't Grow On Trees

JEAN ROSS PETERSON

BETTERWAY PUBLICATIONS, INC.
WHITE HALL, VIRGINIA

Published by Betterway Publications, Inc.
Box 219
Crozet, VA 22932

Cover design by Tim Haley
Text illustrations by Chuk Batko, Rowdy Creative, Inc.,
Minneapolis, MN

Library of Congress Cataloging in Publication Data

Peterson, Jean Ross
    It doesn't grow on trees.

    Includes index.
    1. Finance, Personal--Study and teaching
2. Children--Finance, Personal--Study and teaching.
I. Title.   II. Title: It does not grow on trees.
HG179.P443   1988   649'.63   88-2885
ISBN 0-932620-96-5 (pbk.)

Printed in the United States of America
9 8 7 6 5 4 3 2 1

To my parents, Helen and Charles Ross,
who gave me a financial education.

Author's Note

Will your child swim laps the first time he gets his feet wet? Do you expect your child to be a downhill racer before she masters the snowplow?

It is equally ridiculous to anticipate your youngsters will someday know what to do with a thousand dollars if they have not first practiced with fifty cents. Yet as parents, we shy away from conscious and purposeful instruction in the one area essential to sustain achievement in all others: MONEY!

And that is what this book is about: how to take a healthy attitude toward money, combine it with some cents, and have your child put them both into daily practice so he or she is equipped to succeed when faced with the choices in adult life.

Hundreds of children and parents wrote this book. Educators, bankers, brokers, psychologists, psychiatrists, and economists contributed their words. I added my experiences as a parent, a schoolteacher; as a lecturer and writer in adult financial matters. I am indebted to all the generous and gracious men, women, and children who let me use their knowledge so you can create a financial education for your children.

Before reading this book, you should know I make no effort to use feminine and masculine pronouns in equal number. Any child is every child, and it is children who are important.

Acknowledgment

Katherine K. Baptie is a major contributor to this book. Her energy, inspiration, indeed, many of her words shape the content.

I am most grateful for her generous and invaluable contributions.

Contents

1.
Here Today, Gone Tomorrow

A late night drive alone on a deserted freeway gave me plenty of time to consider why a class in personal finances left me, the teacher, sad, sympathetic, and very angry. By the time I reached my exit, the reason was clear: every man and woman sitting in the classroom was, in some way, a victim of financial abuse. And I was angry because it need not happen to anyone!

The impact of debt at every level

Obviously there are varying degrees of financial abuse, but in the extreme, it is no less harmful to the well-being of an individual than is any other form of abuse in our society. However, unlike others, financial abuse is easily prevented; the prevention requires no great expenditures of time, effort, or money; and it does not demand education or treatment by professionals. As a parent, you have the qualifications and the opportunity to ensure that your children grow up without experiencing the devastating effects from the ignorance which leads adults into destructive financial decisions. Believe me. Your youngsters will not learn all they need to know any place other than at home.

Should you think I exaggerate the harmful effects of imprudent judgments about money, take a moment to review some of the evidence. Debt in our society — the individual debt of consumers and farmers, the institutional debt of banks, the collective debt of our federal government — threatens the stability of our nation. Naive dependency upon Social Security to support an increasing population of elderly places economic burdens upon every wage earner. For the first time in the history of the United

States, economists predict an erosion in our standard of living; it is questionable whether your children will attain the standard reached by their grandparents.

Subsequent chapters will show you the specific lessons you can teach your children so they achieve financial literacy before they leave home. The title of this chapter, "Here Today, Gone Tomorrow," states the unavoidable truth about children: eventually they do grow up and leave home. Both their failures and accomplishments will result from how, when, and why they make decisions. True, each decision will be theirs, and you cannot intervene in the lives of your adult children, but the skills they will use to reach their decisions are the same skills you give them now while they are growing up.

This chapter's title also describes the financial situation of the men and women sitting in my classes: the money they have today is gone tomorrow (actually, it went), but there the similarity ends because this situation is avoidable. These adults who grew up without a financial education tell me, "If only I had learned about money when I was young, I wouldn't be in this mess now."

Financial abuse; an extreme example

An example of extreme financial abuse comes from one of my students. Larry's parents gave him every advantage while he was growing up. He attended an excellent private school, went to camp in the summer, enrolled in a prestigious university, graduated, was married, and went to work in his father's company. Six years later, his father died and the company was bought out by a competitor. As a result, Larry inherited close to a million dollars. "It didn't take me long to lose it," he told me, "and now, even with my wife working, I'm worried about how I'm going to put our kids through college." Larry's story is repeated over and over again by others; the only variant is the amount of money involved.

Very few of us will know we have lost a million dollars because we will never have that much money in our hands at any one time. Given sufficient time and prolonged ignorance, however, all of us are capable of matching Larry's record loss. The following episode shows you how easy it is to do this when you begin as a young child with small sums of money.

Small change adds up

Aunt Judy came to stay with Steve, a first grader, and his two younger sisters while their parents were on a vacation. The day before the parent's return, Judy gave the house a thorough cleaning, and in the process she found pennies, nickels, dimes, and quarters under sofa pillows and chairs, or lying scattered on shelves and tables. As she cleaned, she stuck this loose change in her pocket. At the end of the day, she showed the children the money she had collected. "Oh, that money isn't worth anything," they told her, "it's only little money." The coins from Judy's pocket amounted to four dollars and eighty-two cents.

Before you teach your children the value of money and show them how to use it, you might want to ponder your own attitudes, values, and emotions regarding this medium of exchange because we all attach more than a dollar sign to it. Frequently we are not exchanging money in our financial transactions but rather, we are distributing emotional messages and trying to fulfill psychological needs.

Money is power

Money is power. It can elect a president, promote a cause, provide an education, entice a reluctant bride or groom, and, as one cynic observes, "A fool and his money are soon invited everywhere." In a family the power play with money as leverage takes place in a variety of activities. Some illustrations come under the heading of what I call a guilt tax. "I gave you a baseball bat and you struck out. " "I gave you piano lessons and you didn't win a prize in the recital." "I'm afraid our summer vacation will be in the back yard this year. We can't afford to send our kids to college and also enjoy the good life. But we don't care — we're happy to sacrifice for our children's futures." "Tommy, your mother and I are pleased we can send you to camp this summer. I expect you to take advantage of everything there — you know, I never went to camp because I had to work all summer when I was your age."

Then there is the retaliation game: "He bought a new power saw; I'm buying a microwave." "She spends a fortune on clothes; I deserve this new fishing gear." "You subscribe to *Sports Illustrated*; I'm ordering *Sunset*."

Probably all of us are familiar with at least one of these next statements.

"I don't want you to tell your father what I paid for your coat." "Don't tell your mother how much we spent at the stamp show." "Why did you buy Sue or Dick that game when we already agreed it is too expensive?" "Honey, I know I haven't spent much time with you lately because of the pressure at the office, so here's a little something for you." "Gee, kids, I'm sorry I can't take you to the (whatever), I have to work this weekend. Here's a twenty for each of you — have a good time."

Money and image

When you step out of the house, it's easy to see how money is used to reinforce or create an image for the person holding the wallet. Clothes and cars are typical symbols exhibited to proclaim "I'm a success." When other drivers see someone in an expensive sports car, it validates the image that person wants to convey and perhaps wishes were true: "I have money, therefore I have power, therefore I am important." The messages from clothing, especially for women, proclaim not only success and prestige but are frequently used to validate self-esteem: "See how much my husband loves me? You know it by the clothes he buys me or the jewelry he gives me, and if you see it, it must be a fact."

The actual dollars are meaningless in all of these examples, for they are simply the means to express power, love, anger, prestige, guilt, or domination, and to attain outward validations of self-esteem and self-worth as substitutes for internal doubts and insecurities. Parents must be sensitive to their own emotional attachments to the dollar or they risk inserting similar feelings into their financial transactions with their youngsters. Now that these danger flags are unfurled to attract your attention, let's look at the beneficial economic encounters you can have with your children.

Include the children in financial discussions

Include your children in family money matters and encourage their participation in your financial discussions. Some parents fear their youngsters will repeat the information at a neighbor's house or in the classroom, but I am not suggesting you show your children an income statement or burden them with undue concerns over debts or financial obligations to the point they have nightmares worrying they may not have food or shelter. You can explain, even to little ones, that some information is only for the family and not to be shared with others; an occasional slip of the tongue is worth the risk because children need to feel they are an active part of the family, that it is not a case of "them and us." Furthermore, children should know there are limits to family finances or they will confuse "we can't afford that" with "they don't want me to have it." The first statement is a realistic and objective assessment of a situation, while the other carries an emotional message. The more emotions we can remove from our dollars, the more rational we are in how we use them.

Children involved in the decision-making process are less likely to see themselves as helpless victims of dogmatic authority. When they understand the limitations of the family income and have a chance to find what it costs to supply the necessities, they do not act as tyrants making outrageous demands upon their parents' wallets.

Recently I heard a father discuss his emotional and psychological reactions to losing his job when his company declared bankruptcy. He spoke of the stress it put on his marriage and described his feelings of inadequacy and failure as he completed his third month of job interviews. His story is sad, but his final statement is pitiful: "Of course I do everything I can to shield my kids from this. I want them to think nothing has changed, but I don't know how I'm going to keep up our membership in the tennis club or get the new skis they expect. My son wants a car for his next birthday."

Surely this man's children are not ignorant of the tension between their parents. Certainly they know dad isn't on an extended vacation. Kids are not stupid! Yet this father denies his children an opportunity to give him love and support. Furthermore, when he attempts to hide reality, they conjure up possible causes for family stress that are far more disturbing to them than temporary financial adversity. Children included in discussions of family finances can be reasonable, understanding participants; by being involved, they feel valued, which in turn fosters a healthy sense of self-worth, a major psychological strength they use every day.

Security that comes from limitations

Today all children, regardless of the financial circumstances in their homes, grow up in stressful environments. Their increased opportunities mandate additional choices; the pressures of our consumer-oriented society necessitate sophisticated scales to evaluate available options. Youngsters need and want the security that comes from limitations they don't have to set for themselves. When five dollars is the limited income, they don't have to fret about what to do with fifty. Young consumers learn how to successfully function within the limitations set by their parents; in accomplishing this, they also find out they are not passive or ineffectual, but are decision-makers with control over their environments and themselves. These children adopt the attitude: "Hey, I'm more then OK, I'm terrific!" Moreover, kids need to find out they can make a "crummy" decision and the world (and their parents) won't descend on them. When you survive an error, you do not fear the risk of failure, but you have a sharper sense of the difference between a risk and a gamble. Children who are raised with an endless supply of silver spoons never find out what you have to earn to buy one, have no incentive to search for a new one, and, my goodness, they never consider building a silver spoon factory so they can market the product to others. Let's raise children who are independent and proud of their own standards, who evaluate their failures and successes with equal honesty, and who face the world assured of their own abilities.

Financial education; no discrimination by sex

So far, my comments have focused on children, plural. The plural includes both boys and girls. Is there a parent anywhere who discriminates between his or her children? Or who believes girls should be excluded from a financial education? A sad commentary on the fate of girls who were denied the skills to manage money are the statistics that point to the main reason women stay in abusive and destructive marriages as being their fear of economic independence and survival. The only reason I bring this up at all is a nagging little worry I have that came to me as I interviewed children and parents for this book.

Because I interviewed minors, and because the subject was money (always a suspect topic), I was particularly careful to ask permission first from parents; if at all possible, I preferred that the parents sit in on the conversations. But my observations bother me. When both parents were in attendance, it was the father who listened carefully, asked questions, and offered comments for either his son or daughter. The mothers were passive observers and did not get involved in the discussions. Yes, their children received equal allowance, the same opportunities, identical responsibilities for chores and work at home, but the fathers dominated the financial discussions. Children pick up on these signals; despite the fact that Johnny and Mary both receive five dollars a week, both cut the grass and wash the dishes, I wonder if money still has sex in it. Please, try to turn your dollars into a neuter gender so we do not perpetuate the prejudice against little girls and hinder them from becoming the independent, unafraid women we want them to be. If yours is a two-parent family, you may want to take the following money/sex test. Which parent says: "I talked to my broker today."; "Have you talked to your broker this week?"; "It's time for me to figure out the income tax return."; "The bank statement came and I can't get it to balance with the checkbook."; "We should evaluate our insurance policies."; "I'm buying one hundred shares of XYZ first thing tomorrow!"?

Parents: United you stand!

Another caution for two-parent families involves the need to stand united in financial decisions affecting your youngsters. If you disagree, settle the matter in private conversation; otherwise, the children will quickly catch on that your divided opinions are the breach into which they can thrust their empty piggy banks.

By now you may have figured out that I consider money one of the less important ingredients in a child's financial education. The goal is not wealth; not to teach your children how to become millionaires. (Should that happen, however, we will not have failed.) The objectives are the attitudes and values you instill in your youngsters so they leave home confident and skilled in their abilities as independent adults.

Accountability

Before you turn to the details on how to achieve these objectives, there is one more word we cannot ignore: *accountability*. It isn't used much anymore, at least I never see or hear it, and I suspect its unfashionable status is one reason we have so many youth problems in our society today. We hear about peer pressure, unfortunate environments, lack of opportunity, and inferior educations as excuses for incompetence, failure, or worse. Somehow the idea of accountability has become lost among the horde of extrinsic culprits. I hope, though, that we can return it to our children, for it serves as a responsible motivator. When you teach your sons and daughters how to use money, you bring accountability into their lives as they learn there is no one else they can fault or praise for their financial decisions. Whether we want to or not, each of us accepts responsibility for what we do with our money, because ultimately we cannot escape the consequences.

2.
Make Allowances for Children

My father's income is Social Security and a pension. My daughter's is a salary. The IRS, with a wisdom based on fairy tales, labels my income as self-employed, despite my conviction it belongs in the category of insufficient funds.

While these designations for adult incomes are generally accepted without debate or controversy, a child's income — the allowance — not only raises questions, but frequently eyebrows and hackles. It is my hope that by raising questions and suggesting answers to the allowance dilemma we can eliminate the negative side effects of a child's income.

The first question is one of definition. What is an allowance? It is a designated portion of the family resources, distributed to a child on a regular basis, and granted with a permit for its reasonable use. In other words, it's the cash you give your kids, when you give it, how much you give, and what they will do with it.

Audrey G. Guthrie, a specialist in consumer education and family management at West Virginia University, directed an extensive research program on the subject. In her "Children Learn Money Management" program, she surveyed over four hundred households, including almost one thousand children. I asked Professor Guthrie for her conclusions based on the results of the project and for her observations of family money management.

"I see no direct relationship between a child's ability to manage money and the financial situation of the family," she said. "It is the values and patterns of the family that are the greatest influences. The way in which a child uses money is set by the parents in the preschool years. By the time a child is in high school, it is too late."

A financial education starts with an allowance

My experience leads me to the same conclusions, though with somewhat greater optimism. An effective financial education is possible at any age, but, like skiing, the younger you start, the better the chances you will master all the maneuvers. I cannot find one authority who does not agree with Professor Guthrie: the best way to give your children a financial education is to give them an allowance!

In spite of the differences among adult incomes — their designations and sources — and regardless of the contrast between the income for an adult and the allowance income for a child, there is an intrinsic mischief in all incomes: they are limited. If your children can learn that income is finite by rehearsing with an allowance before they reach the adult stage in life, perhaps you can spare them the turmoil and wretched consequences endured by someone like Stan.

Stan sent me his horror story in a letter. (The name is changed to protect the guilty.)

"I'm thirty-four years old, single, and make one hundred thousand dollars a year. I have car payments, a second mortgage, and debts that total about eighty thousand. My savings are zero. Please help! P.S. I'll write you a year from now and we'll see how it looks."

Stan's letter struck my sympathetic nerve, albeit with a discordant whack. When I responded to his written request with a telephone call, he volunteered a brief, yet significant history.

"Stan," I asked, "When you were a child, did you have an allowance?"

"Sure, but you know what I did? When I was six, the day I received my allowance I spent it all on candy. When I was thirteen, I bought hamburgers. At twenty-one, I was in the Navy and every payday was followed by a night on the town."

You can't fault Stan for inconsistency! He still has a few more months to work on his financial reclamation project, so I can't give you his year-end chapter. However, he checks in with me now and then to report on his progress and we're both optimistic. Completed or not, Stan's story carries a warning label for every allowance. Caution: unless accompanied by a parent's prescription for reasonable use, money will have harmful side effects for children.

An allowance alone is not enough

Obviously, Stan received only one part of his allowance: the cash. His parents forgot the financial education that gives an allowance its true value, and lets a child learn the consequences of indiscriminate spending and debt, as well as the rewards from constructive financial decisions. Before we look at the beneficial ways to give a child an allowance — the when, how much, what for ways — let's consider the alternative, which I call the "handout" method.

Every time your child needs or wants money, he has to beg, plead, wheedle, or cajole to get some. Frankly, I think that's a rotten way to treat a child. He can't make one decision without your approval. His plans depend on your unpredictable responses. Imagine how you would feel if every time you wanted to buy a magazine you had to get permission from your wife or husband. Your conversation might go as follows:

"Dear, may I have two dollars?"

"What for?"

"A magazine."

"What's the name of it?"

"*Business Week.*"

"Why do you want to read that one? I think *Newsweek* is better."

"But all my friends read *Business Week*, and"...and on, and on, and on.

Allowance, yes; handouts, no

When you must justify each action and decision in your daily life, pretty soon you catch on to what the person in control thinks of you. It's not much. With a parent in total financial control, a child's income based on the "handout" method transmits insidious messages. In effect you are telling him: "You are dependent. Your ideas and choices are good only when I say they are. You can't be trusted to make a decision. Always look to me for approval. You are powerless and I am in control."

These are examples of authoritarian parenting, which usually produce a child (and then an adult) incapable of solving a problem or making a decision. Unfortunately, some children recover from parental instruction in dependency only when, years later, their income floats a psychiatrist's yacht.

Furthermore, the "handout" method of income distribution isn't all that great for the parent. He is constantly hassled by requests for money and then badgered for still more money. Instead of teaching his child how to manage money, he is teaching his child how to manage a parent. Children do not need additional training in this skill; they are born with it. What parent (in his right mind) wants to encourage tears and tantrums in exchange for dollars? The sane alternative is an allowance that includes the benefits of a financial education.

Now that we have settled the definition and substantiated the purpose of an allowance (I trust!), the next question I want to raise is the matter of timing. At what age should your child begin his allowance education?

Children as young as three or four know it takes more than a lick and a promise to enjoy an ice cream cone: it takes cash. At this age, a child may not understand the comparative or numeral value of coins, but he can learn to exchange them for the things he wants. He'll know which coin buys gum, or that it takes two of the little ones (dimes) and two of the big ones (quarters) before he chooses strawberry. Nor do these young consumers comprehend the progression of time. If you tell a three-year-old on Tuesday that he can have his treat on Saturday, he'll be sadly disappointed when you don't take him to the store Wednesday morning.

But before I say another word about small children and money, I must sound a warning bell. If your child takes the word "consumer" too literally, he should not have money in his hands. I was fortunate when my child was very young — she never put money in her mouth. She preferred leaves. One parent told me how a family tradition teaches her children about money in a "Look, but don't touch" method.

"Each new baby in our family receives a framed set of coins, minted in the year of his birth. My grandfather began this tradition for his children, and it continues down through the generations. When the children are old enough to talk and listen to stories, they love to look at their money, hear the names of the different coins, and see their birthdate printed on the money. By the time they are old enough to safely handle money, they can recognize each coin by name and tell how much it is worth."

I think this is a delightful tradition; in fact, I'm going to borrow it to use from now on in my own family.

Start them young

I believe a financial education should begin when a child is old enough to say, "Buy me...I want...," whenever you take him into a store. His first allowance, however, should be based on an event rather than on the calendar. Instead of giving your three-year-old a quarter every Monday, associate his allowance with the family schedule and define the amount by an item you consider reasonable for his consumption.

Rebecca is a financial planner and mother of two children, aged three and five. I asked her to tell me how she handles the allowances for her young consumers.

"I do my major shopping once a week and the kids know that the only time they can have a treat is when we are in a store. I don't want them to have gum or candy, so I let each child pick out his favorite piece of fruit, or choose one of those little packs of peanut butter crackers. When we are in the check-out line, I let the children hold their own treats, show them to the checker, and find out how much they cost. Then I give each child enough money so he can pay for his purchase himself. The children know these treats are never eaten in the store, but are to be saved until we get home."

"But what do you do when your children see other kids eating candy or cookies while shopping with their mothers?" I asked.

"I just tell them our family doesn't spend money on things like that, and we don't eat anything before we pay for it."

Rebecca has strict limitations on the things her children can select as treats. She does not hesitate to tell them that not *every* family has the same values or follows identical behavior patterns.

I would not be as strict as Rebecca. I think a child can chew gum (preferably sugarless), and I see nothing wrong with an occasional candy bar. But I do admire her method.

Louise, a full-time mother of a four-year-old, has a more flexible schedule, so her child is in a variety of stores several times each week. Here is the way she helps her preschooler manage his allowance:

Learning budget limitations early

"I didn't want Tommy to expect a treat — candy, toy, or whatever — every time we went into a store so I told him he could have his very own money once a week and could pick out two things to buy — one treat and one toy. He knows about money because I show him the coins, tell him their names, and try to explain what each coin is worth. When I do my weekly shopping, he can choose one treat. We talk about what it costs, and I help him count his money to see if he has enough to pay for it. I let him pay for his own treat when we go through the check-out line. Then the other thing he can buy — when we are in toy stores or drugstores — is something small, maybe a balloon, stickers, or other little things like that. But he knows he must pay for it himself, and I help him decide what he can afford. I always buy him books — he doesn't ever have to pay for those. For his birthday, I gave him a little bank and he keeps his allowance money in there until it's time for his shopping day. Most of the time this works out, but sometimes he wants a toy that costs a dollar when he has only fifty cents. It's hard not to give in and hand him the difference, but then I think about all the things I can't afford, and I guess he's learning you can't buy everything you want."

Both of these mothers, Rebecca who is a financial planner, and Louise who works at home, are giving their children much more than coins when they go shopping. Their children are getting a feel for money, both literally and figuratively.

One way you can help your children learn about money is to let them play "store" at home. When my child was preschool age, I collected large cardboard boxes from an appliance store and stacked them along the wall of the garage or basement. I helped

CAN I BUY IT?

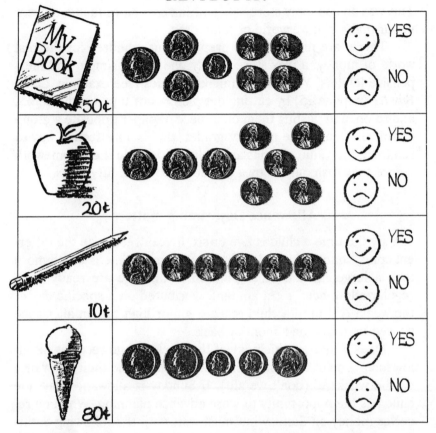

my daughter wrap some inexpensive shelf-liner paper around the sides and front of the boxes and paint a "store" sign on the front. Under the sign she pasted pictures of food and toys which she had cut out from our old magazines. I saved empty boxes from food, soap, drugstore items, cleaning products — any kind of packaging that couldn't cut little fingers. Together we made price signs from heavy paper or cardboard and she used tape to fasten the prices to the boxes. This play store was very popular with her and her friends, especially on rainy or snowy days. Once in a while, as a surprise, I would add a real item to the store: a box of raisins, a small box of dried cereal, even a bit of candy now and then. The play money was made of circles cut from various colors of stiff paper; I put both the numbers and the names of the coins on each circle. A red circle was **1** on the front and **one** on the back; blue was five; yellow was ten; and green was twenty-five. This was an economy store — nothing cost more than a quarter in our make-believe world of commerce.

There are many ways to prepare your children for the real world of money; a play store is only one of the simple and inexpensive lessons. You also can make puzzles (see example, *Can I Buy It?* on page 25) by cutting out pictures of toys, candy, books, and so on, and pasting them on a piece of paper opposite a group of coins. Even in the primary grades, this is an effective way to reinforce the value of coins and help children do their homework before they rush out to buy a two-dollar toy with fifty cents.

Allowance Day; timing matters

By the time a child is five or six, he can recognize the different coins, count, add, and realize that a small dime is worth more than a larger nickel. Most children at this age are ready for a regular allowance: a set amount distributed on a specific day of the week. Not until a child reaches junior high can an allowance be well-managed on a monthly basis.

Does it matter which day of the week a child receives his allowance? I believe it does. Children usually spend their allowance on the weekend (don't we all!). If Sunday is allowance day, the child has the opportunity to learn advance planning. When he receives money on Sunday but must wait until the following Saturday to spend it, he's also learning about delayed gratification. (Do you remember the story of my poor friend Stan, who wrote to me asking for help? He is still paying the price for his childhood habits of immediate gratification.) I'm sure you know some adults who, as children, blew all their allowance on bubble gum, and today rush a paycheck to the bank to cover the installment debt on a BMW they must drive now, never later. One mother I talked to said she gives her six-year-old fifty cents every Sunday evening. During the week, her child cuts out pictures of things she wants to buy when they go shopping on Saturday, and she keeps her "cut-out plans" on the refrigerator door. "The pictures change almost as frequently as the door opens," her mother said, "and I help her figure out whether or not she can afford her choices so when Saturday arrives, she has realistic expectations."

Be consistent, not manipulative

No matter which day of the week you pick as allowance day, it is your responsibility to have the exact amount of money ready to hand over to your child. You might even pick a certain time of day, perhaps at dinnertime. Why is this important? Our kids do to others what we do to them. If a parent forgets to give an allowance or has a ready excuse for not having the money available, the child learns it's OK to forget to make his bed or not finish his homework because he had to babysit for a little sister. Can you imagine your reaction if your boss told you on payday that your check wasn't ready because he was busy entertaining some out-of-town guests? Tom Kreilkamp, a child psychologist at the Harvard Medical School, says, "No matter what decision you reach about when to give your children allowances, *be consistent!* Money should never be used to manipulate a child's behavior."

An allowance given on a regular basis is a terrific bargain. For fifty cents on Sunday at dinnertime, your child receives complimentary lessons in punctuality, reliability, consistency, and dependability. All this, and without those boring lectures!

How much allowance?

So far, in our discussion of the timing for an allowance — when to begin one, when to distribute the money — I use fifty cents as an example of the base amount upon which future increases will build. The question of how much allowance to give a child causes dissention in many families. No parent wants to give an allowance that is drastically lower or higher than an amount that suits the family budget and meets the child's requirements. Naturally, the primary consideration for determining the amount of an allowance is the financial situation of the family. In many families, especially where there are several children, allowances could add up to over fifty dollars a month for the parents (I gasp at the thought!). This may be a burden the parents cannot afford to carry.

Another consideration is the area in which the family lives. A child who lives in New York City, rides in taxis, and pays big-city prices for necessities as well as for pleasures will have financial needs far different than a child living in, say, Broken Arrow, Oklahoma. The latter child can take a bus, go to a neighborhood matinee, or ride his bike to a club meeting.

In addition to the family's income, size, and living environment, there is the question of exactly what items a child will pay for with his allowance.

Last year on a flight between California and Minnesota, I sat between two people with opinions as identical as those states. My seatmates covered the miles with their conversation about the best way to give children some money.

Two different approaches

Mary, on my left, grew up in a small town; her parents were hard-pressed to raise their children on a less than modest income. Every week, each child received a nickel to spend on anything she chose. Now Mary has five children of her own and they receive an allowance until they finish high school. "I'll never forget," she told us, "how I felt when I walked into a store and knew I could spend my pennies on anything I wanted. In those days, a nickel bought a lot of candy. I guess I was born to shop. I pay for everything my children need — school supplies, lunches, music lessons, club dues, sports, clothes — but they use their allowances for things they want. It's their money and I want them to enjoy it."

Howard, on my right, was eager to give us more than his two cents worth on this subject. As you will see from his story, this was a unique gesture.

Howard grew up in a rural environment, and his parents were very poor. He had worked for every dime he ever had and, to quote Howard, "Today I am a financial success." He never gives his two sons an allowance. "Kids need to learn there is no free lunch. If they need or want something, they should work for it. Both of my boys have regular chores they must do around the house as long as they live under my roof. When they were in the second grade, I started them on additional special projects so they could earn money. Each boy begins the month with five dollars. I assign the special projects. If they are not on time to start a job, I deduct fifty cents. If they gripe about the work, are sloppy in their performance, or dawdle over the job, then each one of these actions means another fifty-cent reduction. At first, my oldest boy earned only one dollar. The next month he made two. From then on, I never had a problem (did they, I wondered?), and both boys always end the month with five dollars. Now they are in high school and I have them save most of their money so they can invest it. Of course, I give them advice on that, too. If they want a car, they know they will have to pay for it. If they use my car, I charge them for gas and their share of the insurance and depreciation. My kids will thank me someday for teaching them how to manage money."

Whew! I mentally thanked the pilot for bringing me down to earth where I had time for only a brief response to my travel companions: good luck.

At any age, too much money is as destructive as too little. Parents constantly walk a tightrope between extravagant and stingy; we all struggle to maintain the perfect balance between what we give and deny to our children.

Some parents give 'til it hurts

From conversations with parents, from my own experience, and from the hundreds of letters and questionnaires I have received, most parents agree: it is easier to give than to withhold. Excessive giving, however, has only short-term rewards for the parent, while it has very long-term penalties for the child.

Do you remember my seatmate, Howard? About the only thing his boys don't pay for is the air they breathe. At the opposite end of the spectrum, I interviewed a young man, twenty-two years old, who has never consumed anything other than free lunch. Stuart is part of a group raised on a diet most of us find unpalatable. He and I had a long conversation (several conversations, in fact); I'll try to report his story as briefly, yet accurately, as I can.

"My folks didn't want to be bothered with an allowance," Stuart told me. "They said it was easier if they just gave me what I needed. And my dad didn't want me to work during the summer because he thinks it's important for kids to learn tennis, golf, and to travel. Anyway, I always went to summer camp and when I got home, it was the only time he could take the family on a vacation. At Christmas we usually went to a resort somewhere. My folks gave me a car when I was sixteen. I have always had a couple of credit cards, so I really don't have to pay for much. When I was in college, I spent summers traveling with friends or working on my tennis at the Club. Dad got me a job with a friend of his when I finished school, but it wasn't much of a challenge, so I quit after a few months. Then I got another job after awhile, but they didn't pay any attention to my ideas, so I left about a year ago. The folks have plenty of room at home, but I wanted my own place. Mom fixed it up for me — even gave me a microwave. Guess she wants me to eat home once in awhile. I get kind of bored during the day, but my friends are available evenings and weekends. I should look for a job, but I'm not sure what I want to do. My folks tell me I shouldn't settle for just any job — my Dad says to wait until the right one comes along. He got me a new car so I don't have to worry about wheels for now."

There is much more to Stuart's story, but I'm sure you don't need (or want) to hear it. What will happen to him when his free lunch is no longer available? And his free dinners, cars, clothes, rent, and recreation? He is one of the most underprivileged people I have ever met; his parents, in my opinion, are guilty of financially abusing their son.

Most of us (unless we are flying) prefer a middle position. As a member of the nonextremist group, you probably place a higher value on the lessons your child learns with his allowance than on the money itself. If the purpose of an allowance is to give children the skills and values for sound money management and effective consumerism (as I believe it is), then a child should use his income for both luxuries and necessities.

What should an allowance buy?

The following chart may help you decide what things your child will pay for with his allowance. It also suggests a practical way to increase your child's financial responsibility as he progresses through the grades.

A	B	C	D
Preschool	**Primary**	**Intermediate**	**Junior High**
	A,	A & B,	A,B, & C,
	plus:	plus:	plus:
treats	gifts	entertainment	clothes
snacks	school supplies	recreation	school activities
toys	charity	school lunches	investments
	hobbies	club dues	
	savings		

It is easy to follow a chart listing the orderly progress of grade levels and their attendant financial responsibilities. Children, as all parents know, are neither orderly nor predictable, so you will want to consider this information only as a suggestion, adapting it to your own situation.

Keeping up with the Joneses

As you increase your child's financial responsibilities, you also must increase his income. This brings us back to the great debate: how much money should I give my child? The answer to this question involves the same considerations we have already discussed: family finances, environment, the size of the family, and the items an allowance will buy. But there are additional influences to think about when you determine the size of an allowance. One of these is an outside influence: your child's friends. It's a good idea to find out from other parents how much money they give their children. None of us finds it comfortable to live in poverty, especially when we are surrounded with riches. On the other hand, a millionaire sticks out like a sore thumb when his associates have incomes like, well, mine for instance. Your chat with "the Joneses" doesn't mean you have to match them dollar for dollar. The information will, however, provide a reasonable defense against the ritualistic negotiation technique used by all children: "Everybody else gets a bigger allowance than I do." And what is the outcome if your child does receive a bit less than his friends? He gets a healthy dose of reality. Life in the real world does not guarantee financial equality for all.

There is yet another consideration, but this is one you should *not* include when you ask, "How much?" I'm talking about your historical evaluation of an allowance. Forget how much money your parents gave you when you were seven, ten, or thirteen. History may repeat itself, but it prints a new price tag for each reappearance. Even the tooth fairy raises the sticker price for her nocturnal visits. In the early 1900s, she replaced the tooth with a dime. By 1950, that same tooth went for a quarter. Today's under-the-pillow magic show produces anywhere from fifty cents to a dollar.

Needs and wants

A practical (not necessarily foolproof) way to determine how much allowance a child needs at each step along the way is to keep a list for a few weeks of the amounts actually spent on items you consider reasonable necessities and luxuries for your child. Then sit down with your child and discuss (not argue!) his expectations. The settlement is a compromise based on reality, one that definitely includes *your* values and goals, as well as his needs and wants. If the compromise can't be worked out, agree to a one-month trial period, during which time your child should keep an accurate record of all his spending. (If I were his parent, I'd keep the same records.) In this way, the allowance level is set by an objective research project (only the government finds it easy to wheedle from statistics).

Once the amount is decided upon, be firm in your resolve to stick with it until the next increase is due. If an allowance always is negotiable, there is little need for the creative process called work. Or for the novel concept called save. Both of these topics — work and save — are essential components in a financial education and will be discussed in subsequent chapters. Because it is a conclusion based upon an allowance, I should mention the results of a survey published in the April/May 1985 issue of *Penny Power* magazine. According to their survey, children who receive an allowance are better savers than those who do not receive a regular "paycheck."

An allowance and chores are not related

An allowance does not have an exclusive right to the term "non-negotiable." Chores (as opposed to jobs) fall in the same category. Just as an allowance is a child's share of the family income, a chore is his share of the family life. Each member of a family performs chores; nobody is paid to do them. They are pretty much the same in all families and equally boring. (Jobs vary significantly from family to family, and they differ in complexity as well as in remuneration.) In any discussion of an allowance, I believe chores should be kept in the closet — under the bed, in a wastebasket, or at the kitchen sink. A child's allowance and his chores are not related, and they should be seen as separate companions in his practice sessions for the adult games he will enter and in which he must compete. Assuming you resolve to keep a steady grip on your child's income, let us now return to the question of a timely change.

Most parents I interviewed feel an allowance should increase each September when the child begins a new grade in school. Summer is a less structured season, kids are excited to see their school friends again, and life returns to a routine. Your child needs new school supplies, new clothes, and, most likely, a new allowance.

At this point, it seems our allowance problems are solved. All you have to do is give your child a "raise" every fall. A conscientious parent gives a dependable child an allowance with an automatic annual increase. End of chapter, right? Wrong.

You can give your child a bike, show him how to ride it, teach him all the safety rules, yet know it is only a matter of time before he rides recklessly down a hill and limps home for Band-Aids and love. If your child is normal, he's also going to have some reckless moments with his money. Let's get out the Band-Aids — and the love — so we are ready to treat the mishaps that occur in the life of every young money manager.

Not all scrapes and bruises, however, will result from amateur or reckless behavior. Some are inflicted by the good intentions of parents (we'll talk about these, too). But now let's begin a series of "what if" situations.

"What if...?"

What if your young child loses his allowance? The first time this happens, I would replace the lost money. Here is an opportunity to turn a short-term loss into a long-term gain (educators call it a learning experience.) Calmly and without censure, ask your child some questions that will lead him to his own answer. For example: "Where did you keep your money?" (Pocket, room, school desk, I don't know.) "If you don't want to lose your money, where is a safe place to keep it from now on?" (A little box, a drawer, I don't know.) "Do you know where I keep my money so I will not lose it?" (Here you may have to give your child some suggestions — maybe he needs a special coin purse or a toy bank.) In a matter-of-fact way, but not as a threat, tell your child you will not replace his money if he loses it the next time. Ask him, "What will happen if you lose your allowance and I don't replace it?" He may need you to supply the answer to this question. ("You won't have any money for one week, not until it is time for your regular allowance.") If there is a "next time," don't destroy his opportunity to participate in one of life's reliable connections: cause and effect. Let your child do without the pleasures in his life. You won't have to preach sermons on carelessness and responsibility. He gets the message every time he sees a friend eat an ice cream cone, chew a piece of gum, or play with a new toy.

If it is an older child who loses his allowance and needs school supplies or money for club dues, what do you do? Assuming this is not the first time he has lost his money, I would introduce him to one of life's deceptive experiences. When you borrow to pay for this week, it is painless. It is not until the next week, on the day of reckoning, that you discover the stinging delayed reaction from the bite of debt.

Yes, I would let my child borrow (but only once or twice!) against his next allowance, and I would put the transaction in writing. Printed proof discourages controversy. One parent told me, "I keep my child's IOU on the kitchen bulletin board. Here it is an objective reminder of his financial responsibility, rather than an emotionally charged exchange with me."

If your child repeatedly loses his lunch money, let him make his own lunch and "brown-bag" it during those weeks. If he frequently loses bus money and cannot ride his bike or walk to school, let him pay for his transportation out of money he earns. The purpose is to show your child that compensation is like the night following the day of carelessness. Your goal is not to exhibit your wrath, equate money with pain and suffering, or to convince your child he is a perpetual "loser."

Are the loans interest bearing?

A child who is old enough to borrow for necessities and understand the repayment of debt is also ready to learn about interest. Since your concern is the quality of his financial education, I would not attempt to impersonate the loan officer at your bank. You might set an interest rate for family borrowing at five cents per dollar each week. (Naturally, what is true for the gosling will also be true for the gander.)

Choices and "reasonable use"

What if...you patiently and thoroughly teach your child how to take care of his money, replace his first lost funds with coins and education, let him borrow from next week so he has the necessities (not the pleasures!) for today, yet he always loses his allowance? It is time to match his money with his maturity.

"Johnny, you'll continue to receive three dollars a week to pay for the things you need (no luxuries!), but I will keep your money for you. We'll make an account book so you can see what you spend, where you spend, and how much is left. I'll hand you the money as you need it, but for now, you are not ready to take care of it yourself. Let's handle your allowance this way for one month. Then I want to put it back in your hands; I'm sure you'll do a better job next month."

This approach is objective rather than punitive. You show your child you prefer he manage his own money and you have confidence in him to succeed. You are giving him some help when he needs it, but are not negating his ability to learn, improve, and reach independence. Further, he knows the limits and the terms; he is not in the limbo of incompetence. Since he will have funds only for his needs, he can earn his wants. Amazing transformations occur when the only way to reach a movie is by walking through a clean garage.

What if...your child uses his allowance in foolish ways? A young child, not yet accustomed to an allowance, might spend all his money the first week on candy. This will not ruin his teeth or health for the rest of his life. He may even binge the second week. If you can resist the temptation to scold, yell, threaten ("I'll take your allowance away if you buy anymore of that junk!"), your child will decide for himself that there are better things to do with money than chew or swallow it. He will see a toy or game he wants and candy will lose its tempting flavor. It's sneaky, but if I had a little one who spent all his cash for candy, I would take him into toy stores quite often. Children must learn to make choices. They must figure out from experiences that have meaning in their own lives that one purchase can have fleeting pleasure (candy), while another (a game) gives lasting satisfaction. (For some children, candy is detrimental to their health. If this applies to your child, he must know he cannot spend his money for sweets; this is an important consideration in the "reasonable use" clause for his allowance. If he fails to observe this restriction, confiscate the candy without removing the allowance. In this way, he still has the opportunity to make choices, but he learns that buying candy, the one limitation you must impose, has less than a fleeting pleasure; it incurs a finite penalty.)

Last winter I used part of my "allowance" for a binge. I joined the sunseekers at a desert resort. One morning by the pool, I chatted with two brothers who had just finished a tennis lesson and were waiting for their parents to take them horseback riding (these were not underprivileged kids!). Chris was ten and in fourth grade.

"Oh, sure, I get an allowance, but it isn't enough," he told me. My dad gives me jobs so I can earn extra money. I started washing the family cars when I was six; now I clean our pool every week and cut the grass. I get some of my money for birthdays and Christmas. See this watch? It cost thirteen dollars, and I bought it myself. I saved a lot of money and I bought a Verbot — seventy dollars — but it broke, and when I took it back, I didn't replace it. They cost too much. I keep my savings in the bank. The money I don't take out until I'm sixteen Dad matches, dollar for dollar. I have only sixty-one dollars and seventy-five cents now, but I used some of my savings for our vacation."

"What do you do with your money?" I asked his younger brother, who was seven.

"I buy candy and toys," he said. End of interview.

Chris, the older brother, looked at Jimmy and said, "You're lazy. You do dumb stuff with your money and never save any of it."

Even if your child doesn't have an older brother like Chris to set an example and give advice, the day will come when he doesn't spend all his money on "dumb stuff."

Incentives to save

One of the parents in Audrey Guthrie's "Children Learn Money Management" program sought her advice for a similar situation. "I have two children, one ten and the other a twelve-year-old. My youngest is an excellent money manager; the other is not content until every dime is spent." Guthrie asked the parent, "What is this child doing *without*?" The parent replied, "You know, I never thought about that." According to Guthrie, "A child needs an incentive for conserving money."

When there are several children in a family, they may share a common incentive. They may want an aquarium, outdoor play equipment, a new TV — some item that will benefit the entire family. One parent I interviewed explained how incentives created the "allowance pool" at their house.

"The kids (ages seven to fourteen) came to us with a request for a VCR. We told them it was a good idea, but it wasn't in our budget right now. At one of our family 'conference nights,' I proposed a solution: if each child chipped in part of his allowance, we'd add our money, too. Each week my wife and I contribute five dollars, the older kids put in one, and the younger ones add fifty cents. This 'allowance pool' is now a family tradition. We use it for vacation plans, shares of stock the children want to buy, a special weekend trip, or whatever."

It seems to me these parents have found an ideal way to encourage their children to forego the "dumb stuff." Such an "allowance pool" would work in any family, even when there is one parent with one child. In some respects, it is the same incentive adults find attractive when an employer provides a company savings or investment plan and offers to match employee contributions. Children are not the only ones who need incentives in order to make reasoned choices within the limits of an income.

Bite your tongue

What if...your child uses his allowance in harmful and destructive ways? When I taught elementary school, I discovered one of my students giving his money to classmates. His parents and I discussed the problem; fortunately, they recognized it had nothing to do with money. This lonely child was trying to buy friends. (Without the perceptive intervention of his parents, he could have become an adult who tries to buy love.) These parents did not withhold their son's allowance while helping him improve his social life, but they did intrude their authority into his misguided decisions. There are special times when a parent cannot wait for a child to learn from his own experiences.

What if...you have an older child who reaches a financial decision that is not necessarily harmful, but is outrageously expensive and wantonly extravagant? I can't presume to know your reaction, but this is when the discomfort from my "bitten tongue" turns into excruciating agony. Can we ever quite forget the source of our children's income?

"I work hard for my money and you squander it. You don't appreciate the value of a dollar. Easy come, easy go. You're spoiled. Why, when I was your age...You must think money grows on trees." Do these phrases bring back memories? Most of us have heard them; many of us repeat them to our own children. I think they work the same magic cure as "help starving children by eating everything on your plate." The curative process that does work for me is a combination of faith and reason. I put my faith in the words of the renowned educator, John Dewey, who in essence said, "Children learn by doing." I add reason by weighing the difference between present and future cost. A twenty dollar stupidity at age fourteen is a bargain compared with a two thousand dollar error at forty.

I'm chagrined to let you know the misery I caused my parents when I was fourteen, but I cannot think of a better example. (Even if the shoe doesn't fit, let your child wear it.) I saw a pair of black patent leather shoes with four-inch heels no thicker than my finger. How I coveted those shoes! They cost more than my parents spent on luxuries in an entire month. My parents tried to dissuade me from my stupidity, but I was beyond reason — I was "hell bent for leather." I saved my allowances. I hoarded birthday checks, weeded flower beds, walked dogs, fed cats, and cleaned rabbit cages. Ah, my beautiful new shoes. I winced and tottered my way through a party, salved my blisters for weeks, and never wore the shoes again. My wise and loving parents not once said, "We told you so." The discomfort from those elegant black shoes has led me to and from many a financial decision in my adult life.

Advise and consent

It is an almost irresistible temptation for us as parents to insert our mature judgment as a buffer between our children's immature decisions and the unfortunate consequences they will suffer. Parents yearn to protect their children! Regrettably, the more decisions you make for your child, the less your child learns about decision-making — good, bad, or indifferent. Obviously, this does not mean you deny your child the benefit of your advice. You can point out the pros and cons, offer suggestions, and cross your fingers. The more information you can provide, the easier it is for your child to make an informed choice. Don't you seek advice from your accountant, broker, and perhaps your lawyer, before you make a major financial decision? I do, all the time. But we should make it clear to our children that the final decision is theirs — emphasize they are also entitled to the consequences. (My broker has yet to volunteer his paycheck in exchange for my enthusiastic and brilliant investment debacles.)

When the consequences are traumatic — as with a toy that breaks as soon as your child brings it home, a product that fails to meet advertised expectations, or my own shiny black shoes — a parent is there to commiserate, not recriminate (and certainly not to financially compensate!). An "I told you so" only serves to humiliate a child or belittle his judgment. "Surprise! Look what I have for you," are words that wipe out a memory that would otherwise assist future decisions. Let your child know it's OK to make a mistake (haven't you made one, maybe two, yourself?). Point out how much he has learned and how lucky he will be to know better next time. Help him analyze the error (if he does not already understand why he is miserable) and figure out how he can avoid repeating it in the future.

Praise, praise, and praise again

What if...the consequences of his decision are not a disaster, but turn out to be a success? Here is one time when you, the parent, can hurl yourself into your child's independent financial decision. Praise, praise, and praise again! Generous accolades for your child's actions will put stars in his eyes and thoughts in his head he will never forget.

Last week I was waiting in the teller's line at my bank. I watched a boy complete his transaction, and as he walked past me, I stepped out of line, introduced myself, and asked if I could interview him. His mother was waiting for him, so she listened as we talked (remarkable mother!). He was thirteen, I discovered, and his name is Geof (he told me to spell it that way).

"I do all my own banking," Geof said. "I can't remember when I didn't take care of my own money. My folks give me an allowance, but I have a paper route and I'm saving most of that money. I always check to make sure the teller credits my deposits right, and I watch to see how much interest they pay me."

I congratulated Geof on his excellent money management skills. "You do a better job taking care of your money than many adults I know."

I have not forgotten the look on that young man's face as he turned to his mother and smiled. As they left the bank, I saw her give him a hug. I suspect there were more where that came from when his father heard about this.

3.
Rewards
and Penalties

In the previous chapter, the situations focus on the various ways children use or abuse their allowance income. Now I want to shift the attention to children's report cards, and the uses and abuses parents construct in an effort to improve a child's grades. This shift from money to grades is not as abrupt as you might think; in many families, the two topics are as remote as the child and the television set.

Paying for grades just doesn't work

What if...your child's grades placed him at the top of his class last year, but this term his schoolwork is average? Some parents have such faith in a dollar bill they believe it can turn a C into an A. I cannot state absolutely that this will never happen. But I can rely on the research, studies, and observations of experts in childhood education who say, without exception, that there is no indication a child's grades will improve when he is paid money or given a reward for scholastic achievement. Oddly enough, offering a "bribe" has a negative effect — just the opposite of what one would expect. Sanford Dornbush, professor of sociology and education at Stanford University and director of the Stanford Center for Youth Development, currently directs a research project to investigate the relationship between classroom performance and children's motivations. This study of over eight thousand students shows that children who receive extrinsic rewards or punishments for grades eventually have lower scholastic performances than children motivated by the internal desire to learn. When privileges are restricted in an effort to increase grades, there is little or no improvement. In fact, achievement is less. What does seem to work, says Dornbush, is "subtle praise, assistance, and encouragement." Citing an experience from his own youth, Dornbush, recalls, "One time I was reading a novel because I wanted to read it. I enjoyed the book until, by coincidence, it was assigned as required reading in a class; then I lost all pleasure in the reading." He goes on to explain, "Students who are offered a reward for grades concentrate on the reward and lose satisfaction in the experience of learning."

Professor Herbert Leiderman of the Stanford Department of Psychiatry classifies parents into four groups: authoritarian (demands obedience), permissive (makes few demands for mature behavior), authoritative (sets clear standards and enforces rules but also encourages discussion and the child's independence), and inconsistent (vacillates between permissive and authoritarian). It is interesting to note that children with the least successful school performance have inconsistent parents; children with authoritative (not authoritarian) parents perform the best.

In summary, according to these experts, we see that bribes or threats will not improve grades, and parents who are both consistent and authoritative provide the best motivations for their children.

Not only that, it robs the child of his achievement

My personal opinion on the relationship between money and grades coincides with this Stanford study. In addition to these assertions, I believe a parent who pays a child for his grades is, in reality, robbing him. The child earns his grades through his own efforts: he studies, he learns, the success is his. When the parent steps into classroom and says, "Congratulations on getting an A in English — here is five dollars," does he expect his child to say, "Thank you?" Thank you for what? The parent is neither the student nor the teacher. He did not earn the grade; he did not, with objective evaluation, reward the effort with an A. Yet the parent intrudes in a way that makes his child owe him appreciation and a debt of gratitude. Do you know what I think this accomplishes? It is just one more way the parent maintains control over his child, saying, in effect, "No matter how well you do in school, no matter what you achieve on your own, regardless of your success, you are beholden to me and here is five dollars to prove it."

Scholastic achievements are not measured in dollars

Often in these chapters, I refer to the concept of cause and effect, and the importance it has in a child's financial education (life, for that matter!). When you reward your child with money, privileges, or gifts for his academic performance, you confuse the cause and effect relationship. Your child has a misplaced goal identification. He thinks: "I am in school to give satisfaction to my parents and to obtain rewards for myself." The exclusive and significant purpose of education — learning — is obscured by material and emotional rewards or punishments. Furthermore, when the worth of a child's achievements is weighed in dollars, he tends to take the same scale into his adult life.

It is no coincidence we live in a society that respects and reveres the size of an income but discounts the values and character of the person who spends it.

Moreover, there are some children who rank "4" or "5" in the classroom, but are "10s" when they step away from their desks. Many outstanding children do *not* follow a rigid pattern of A,B,C. These are obviously bright, capable children; when they are penalized for less than maximum performance in school, it may serve to squelch their natural talents and abilities.

I am reminded of Brian who enrolled in my class and brought with him a written evaluation from his former school. "Brian shows immature behavior and may not be ready for second grade. His attention span is limited. He performs at below average in reading and arithmetic."

His teacher was right. Brian did not read his "Dick and Jane" because he was busy studying the directions in a library book for the construction of a terrarium. He did not turn in his "add and subtract" homework because he spent the evening playing chess with his father — he usually won, his father admitted. (A winner at chess with a limited attention span? Hmmm...)

I am also reminded of Chris whom I first met when he was in junior high. His report cards were less than admirable. He had received a D in English, yet spent many afternoons at my kitchen table discussing autobiographies and novels, classic and modern. His math grades were a mix of C and D marks, yet his weekends and evenings were absorbed with calibrations and computations to enhance his performance in sailboat races. Chris always had a job, in addition to his regular chores at home. He was conscientious, dependable, creative, and in great demand by employers. He knew more, and accomplished more, than any of his classmates, yet his parents lamented their son's lack of ability and constantly looked for privileges to remove or punishments to add as a way of improving his grades.

Nowhere is it written that all a parent has to do is find a prescription for easy child rearing, and then remember to take the pills. Actually, some are so bitter it is no wonder we resist swallowing them. But when you consider money as a way to treat a child's grades, I urge you first to examine the side effects.

Good behavior should be appreciated, but not with money

Nor is money a beneficial way to treat your child's behavior! Whether he is nice or naughty, when you dangle a dollar bill in front of a child, it leads him into treacherous territory.

Let's reverse the customary preoccupation and look at good behavior and what happens when you acknowledge it with a financial nod. "Tommy, what a nice boy you are to let your little sister play with your toys. I'm going to buy you a special treat tomorrow when we go shopping." Or, "Son, I was proud of you today when you offered to help Aunt Mary carry those boxes to the basement. Here's a dollar — you deserve it."

Well, what does happen? Rather than feeling good about himself, rather than basking in well-earned praise, the child converts his actions into cash. Words like "nice" and "proud" are lost in the loud realization: "Aha. I'm a nice boy and I get a treat. Aha! I'll be nice whenever I want something." Or, "When I'm thoughtful, my dad feels proud, and I get a dollar. Aha! I'll make my dad feel good and I can get plenty of money."

These are not remarkably crass translations. In any episode of "show and tell," the words are dimmed by the vivid impressions of the objects on display. Children who learn to be "good" for a dollar figure out that "perfect" can net real money. I have seen many, many examples of children, all ages, who have mastered the technique of acquiring money or material rewards with their little smiles and calculated gestures. One of the most repugnant examples I have ever had to witness is the "charming and gracious" high school girl who keeps in constant touch with her grandmother. Oh, boy, does she keep the touch constant. The grandmother is in a retirement community and she receives from her doting grandchild: flowers, notes, postcards, little gifts, telephone calls. The high school girl receives, in return, checks. Lots of checks. Once, I had the nerve to confront this girl with her behavior.

"Oh, it doesn't matter. She has plenty of money, and when I'm sixteen, I want her to buy me a car."

Reward with praise and love...not money

When children expect rewards for their good behavior, they go through life asking, "What's in it for me?" These are not the adults who volunteer for community projects, serve on local charity boards, or donate their time or talent to worthy causes and institutions. Furthermore, when parents use money to commend their children, they at the same time deny the children what they need most: a hug, a smile, or a pat on the back, along with plenty of praise and verbal approval. These are the rewards that give a child his self-esteem and build his character. "Praise is the greatest tool in behavior modification," writes B.F. Skinner, the internationally recognized expert on behaviorism. "It goads us to take risks that expand our lives." Children *are* dependent upon their parents. They know and feel it all the time. So it is up to the parent, the most important person in their lives, to give them the genuine tools for an authentically rewarding and satisfying life.

Since we are not looking at a television family sitcom, there are times when our children are naughty. Not only are they naughty, they are monsters! If only they would use their creative ability for doing the wrong things and instead, direct it into positive actions, we might have world peace, end hunger, eliminate disease — maybe sleep at night.

Alas, they never have, and never will. Reality for parents

means finding constructive ways to turn a toadstool into a mush-room. The first rule, the last rule, and the only rule, is: fit the punishment to the crime.

Punish bad behavior by removing privileges, not the allowance

Don't remove or reduce a child's allowance for any of the following: hitting or kicking his sister, brother, other children, or the cat; yelling, sassing, crying, pouting, swearing; forgetting to clean his room, empty the trash, wash the ring out of the tub, wear his shoes, sweater, coat, or boots; breaking, throwing, smashing, spilling anything — or any of a million other possibilities. In other (and fewer) words, don't mix money with your madness. When our children misbehave, we react like a cat waiting in front of a mousehole: one squeak and we are ready to pounce with claws bared.

Lacking claws, we reach for the handiest weapon, and most of us grab the allowance. But a policy of monetary retribution against children works as well as economic sanctions against foreign terrorists.

What does a child learn from his bad behavior when he is punished with money? He learns he can hit Billy for fifty cents, kick the cat for a quarter, and sass his parents for a dollar, maybe two. At the time, perhaps, to him it is worth it! But what a cruel lesson it is when we fool our children into believing they can get by with anything as long as they have the money to pay for it.

Instead of charging a fine or removing an allowance, a parent can restrict and remove privileges. When your child "forgets" to make his bed, take out the trash, or hang up his clothes, you can give him a reminder by saying, "No friends after school this week; no outdoor play after dinner; no chauffeuring to your friend's house on Saturday." There are long lists of privileges we can remove as ways to enforce proper behavior so our children will not get the idea they can buy their way out of trouble.

Many adults who, as children, missed the connection between privileges and punishments, but learned to judge behavior on a cash-flow basis, view life in the mirrors of a financial fun-house where they see distortions that you and I cannot imagine.

Almost daily the press reports cases of fraud, bribery, graft, or corruption. These stories usually include a sentence about the perpetrator hiring his defense. This is an expensive (possibly ruinous) way to have the legitimacy of cause and effect finally brought to one's attention.

Certainly, I cannot guarantee this is an example of the "treacherous territory" every child will reach if his early behavior is monitored with a dollar, but it is definitely to his advantage (and to ours) to avoid this direction at any cost.

Throughout this chapter and the preceding one, I have tried to illustrate the potentially harmful side effects of a child's income when he receives money without constructive guidance for its use. I hope the illustrations foster preventions that make cures obsolete. It does take an enormous amount of time and patience to teach a child how to manage money and how to value money with a healthy attitude, but the rewards are worth the effort. We can raise a generation who demonstrates that money is not the root of all evil, but rather, it is the resource for great good at home, in the community, and beyond.

4.
Child
Labor

Work is divided into two categories, chores and jobs — a separation distinguished only by one short line: "In God We Trust." Is there any separation between children and adults when we examine the significance work has upon their lives?

INC. magazine reported on a survey of one hundred and fifty entrepreneurs who were asked to divulge the most important influence that gave them the qualities necessary for success. The consensus: the greatest influence came from the home where the mothers required children to help with the chores. (I'm sorry if fathers are offended.) In another study, author A. David Silver investigated the backgrounds of outstanding and singularly productive men and women. His observations, published under the title, *The Entrepreneurial Life*, conclude with the advice: "Make your child self-reliant at an early age."

Self-reliance at an early age

No, I am not suggesting that every child who cleans her room or clears the table will eventually appear in the pages of *INC.*. Nor do I believe a lemonade stand is the immediate blueprint for McDonald's. This is a goal that might serve best when it does not serve at all. Be that as it may...I am convinced the way to a child's full and wholesome development is through her work, whether it is an unpaid chore or a job for a dollar.

Among the experts who investigate all the by-products work creates is John P. Blessing, an educator and a parent. In his book, *Let My Children Work!*, Blessing substantiates the efficacy of chores and jobs when he writes, "If parents always do for a child and act as if he is not able to do it for himself, what kind of ego will he have? We are, in part, what we can do and, if we can do nothing, then we are in part, nothing."

Another authority on the subject of work and its significance in personal development is Dr. Jay Rohrlich, a psychiatrist in the Wall Street community and an occupational psychologist. He states in his book, *Work and Love: The Crucial Balance*, "The feeling of our own reality is enhanced by seeing ourselves defined by our work. Self-esteem is intimately related to the feeling of power...competence means power."

The importance of childhood choices

Do these experts reach the same conclusion? Blessing, writing about children, says work enhances their egos. Rohrlich, directing his remarks to adults, stresses the importance of work in creating self-esteem. These two words, *ego* and *self-esteem*, are interchangeable, and so, it seems, there is no difference between adults and children when it comes to the value work has upon their well-being. Assuming you, too, are convinced that work is an essential activity, let's first look at the practical ways to introduce it to your child through household chores.

Chores begin when your child can pick it up, put it away, fold it, sort it, or carry it out the door. When a chore is turned into a game, even the little ones want to play. "Let's see if we can put all your toys away before the clock reaches five-thirty. Let's take turns: one toy for me, one toy for you." Or, "Look at all these poor little lost socks that tumbled out of the dryer. Let's see if we can help them find their friends. The blue sock finds his. This yellow sock hugs another yellow one." (I, too, like to play these games. Whenever I search for ways to make a chore creative, it becomes less of a "chore.") And your little ones learn much more than how to finish a chore when they play these games with you: they learn, for example, the names of colors, task sharing, counting, telling time, and most important, they learn a positive attitude toward work.

Primary grade children won't be bamboozled by the fun-and-games routines that appeal to preschoolers, but they will respond to praise and encouragement. "You do this (chore) as well as I do — how grown up you are!" "Do you mean to tell me you have cleaned your room already? I can't believe what a good job you did and how quickly you did it. My, you are a good worker!"

Your older children take a more pragmatic approach to chores. They respond well when you use the "carrot in front of the donkey" technique. "We have four chores to finish before I can take you to the library. Which two do you want?" "I want to take you to the pool, but first we must wash the dishes, walk the dog, clean the bathroom, and take out the trash. Let's finish our chores as soon as we can so we have more time to swim."

Once your children reach the age when they know chores are a regular part of their lives and they know how to work independently, you can assign chores by the week or month. Some parents post a chore schedule on the family bulletin board where each child can check off her particular chore as she finishes it.

At every age children need to know certain requirements about their chores. First show your child how to do the task at hand. Be sure she has the necessary equipment and understands how to use it. Let her know your expectations for how long it will take her to complete the chore, the quality of her work, and the consequences of a shoddy or incomplete performance. Obviously, no chore is finished until it meets all the anticipated results.

If your child simply refuses to cooperate, conveniently "forgets" her chores, or consistently has sloppy work habits in spite of your patience and instructions, then it's time to remove or restrict her privileges. Yes, today's work is important, but you are teaching attitudes and habits that will affect her future, and as parents, we cannot afford to be negligent in this, our "teaching chore."

When your children perform their chores, you should occasionally work with them. If Alice sees how you wash the car, she learns by observation the standards you set for yourself and is far more likely to copy what you do than what you say should be done. Finally, when your children work hard and their work is done well, don't stint on the praise. A few words of admiration teach more than a tome of criticism.

Self-reliance leads to self-esteem...

Before we leave our chores and begin to explore the world of work for pay — jobs — I must not fail to mention another significant benefit from the routine tasks we demand of our children, one most of us would never consider and one that adds considerable support and comfort to our endeavors as parents.

...and a sense of self that helps the adolescent assert more control over his life

Dr. Rodney Skager, Associate Dean of Education at UCLA, headed a survey of seventy-five hundred students and found that many youths avoid alcohol and drugs because their self-image prevents the use of these substances. According to Dr. Skager, "If you look back a hundred years, children had chores. They had a function in the family and the accomplishment of those things generalized a real self-esteem." He compares these children with today's youngsters, many of whom lack responsibility and whose sole purpose is to be entertained. When children have a strong sense of who they are, they resist activities culminating in who they aren't.

Unless a family needs the income from every member, including the children, most children begin their job experiences at home. Home is a city apartment, a small-town dwelling, a suburban house, a farm, or a condo. Regardless of the territory, any work exclusive of chores is a potential job. Some of the following suggestions will fit into your domestic scene: polish silver, shovel snow, clean the garage, closets, or a shed; clean outdoor furniture; wash cars, windows, dogs, or yard equipment; haul and stack wood; do yard work; paint; serve and clean up at parties; polish shoes and clean boots, sand and oil wooden tools or kitchen equipment. I'm sure you will find a few jobs for your children from this partial list.

All of the guidelines I've mentioned to promote the best possible results for children when they work at their chores apply equally to their work at a job. But in addition, you must reach for your wallet.

How much for work for pay at home?

How much money should you pay your children when they become your employees? Unfortunately, there is no pay scale to follow when a child cleans the family shoes. Instead, we must use common sense with our tender offers. And our common sense dictates we will not pay our children ten dollars for a three dollar job at home or they will believe the rest of the world eagerly awaits a chance to subsidize their futures. Alas, many children believe this fiction and take it with them into the adult workplace. They expect employers to pay salaries for sloppy work, telephone calls on company time, two-hour lunches, late arrivals and early departures, and numerous recreational activities at water coolers and coffee pots. To prevent your child from entering a fantasy world, practice what I call "tough money." Let her know in advance that if a job does not meet your standards (also defined in advance), she will not receive her salary.

Not long ago, the *Wall Street Journal* ran a series of articles in which children were asked what they expected for their futures. Their typical answers prompt me to investigate foreign investments. "I plan to make a lot more money than my folks do, but I won't have to work as hard to get it." "I want lots of money but I'm not going to break my back." Granted, these children are optimistic now but I wonder if that optimism won't turn into despair when an entry-level position doesn't entitle them to a private secretary within a few years' employment.

It is not uncommon for children to have illusions about the world of work and their places in it, for they see jobs with eyes accustomed to a screening process, whether at the Bijou or in front of a Mitsubishi. My eyes were opened when I interviewed children whose ages ranged from six to fourteen:

Susan, age thirteen: "I'm going to be a model and a fashion designer."

Dave, also thirteen: "I'll be a world class swimmer and a Supreme Court judge."

Eric, age twelve: "I'm going to own hotels and travel on my boat."

Beth, age seven: "Someday I'll be like a famous person on

TV, or a model."

Steve, age eleven: "I want to be a private eye."

Rick, age nine: "I'm going to have my own business, be on a SWAT team, and live on a horse ranch."

This is a random sample from over one hundred children who told me what they intended to do when they grew up. It's interesting to note that when I asked each child if he or she knew how to become whatever occupation was selected, the unanimous answer was, "Go to college."

Truth or consequences

One way you can combat the job myth is to let your children know how you earn your money. If possible, take your children to your place of employment and be explicit when you tell them what you do all day. Encourage them to ask other family members about their jobs. Children who live with illusions and in ignorance about work can suffer serious consequences.

Melinda Stewart, a Juvenile Court judge and the mother of two young children, says of her experience: "Of the hundreds of cases of theft and burglary I see in my Court, by far the greatest number of young offenders come either from families on financial assistance or from families where parents have accumulated wealth that no longer requires them to actively strive to earn money. Underprivileged and overprivileged children both lack role models of hardworking parents; they have no concept of what others do to earn the things they acquire. Therefore, these children have no empathy for their victims, and thus no hesitation or remorse in stealing from them."

To extend your youngster's perception about the ways in which people earn their livings, you can play the following "find a job" game with them when you travel by car. The object is to see who can find the greatest number of different kinds of jobs. Children who know the alphabet can name the jobs in alphabetical order. For example: auto repair, bakery, camera shop, drugstore, electrical shop, farm, etc. Later, as you drive through unpopulated areas, discuss with your children what is done at each job, how many people work there, does the owner work in the building or only the employees, where do they get supplies, when do they open and close, and so on.

Open your child's eyes to the reality of work. There is, after all, a limit to the number of Supreme Court judges and, I would imagine, for models as well.

Junior Achievement programs

Another way in which youngsters are exposed to a variety of occupations is through the excellent programs sponsored by Junior Achievement. This nationwide organization was founded in 1919, and for many years the membership was restricted to students in senior high school. Today, however, Junior Achievement has projects for youngsters in grades four through twelve. Here is another example of specialists in the field of economic education who realized, after considerable experience, that for maximum effectiveness economic education must begin in the lower grades.

Current programs sponsored by Junior Achievement include the following: Business Basics, a class for grades four to six, is taught by the outstanding students in senior high school economic programs. Project Business, a senior high school program, is structured to meet the curriculum requirement in any of the nation's school districts offering credit for courses in economic education.

All children will benefit greatly from participation in Junior Achievement activities. School districts garner tremendous advantages from these programs because Junior Achievement provides free to the district, the textbooks, workbooks, lesson plans, various other materials as well as the teaching staff. And parents have the unique opportunity to make a contribution to economic education when they bring their practical business experience and acumen into the classroom by participating as volunteer teachers. For information write to: Junior Achievement, Inc., 45 Club House Drive, Colorado Springs, CO 80906. Telephone: (303) 540-8000.

In all occupations, in the real job situations, working adults know there is one aspect that never changes: your employer cannot tell you what to do with your paycheck. (He may want to, but job protocol forbids it.)

Once they earn it, it's theirs...within reason

This should also be true for the money your children earn from you, a neighbor, or anyone else. If you demand your children to save all their money, you remove the incentive for them to work. Nor should you remove their allowances just because they have the initiative to work for extra funds. If I had a steady income of forty thousand dollars a year and learned it would be taken away from me because I earned an additional ten thousand, you can bet I wouldn't lift the extra finger. I would continue to work for the ten thousand, however, if I could keep eight thousand but put only two thousand into savings for my retirement. With the cost of a college education reaching astronomical levels, many teenagers will understand a need to save *part* of their earnings if college is their goal.

During the time your children work for you, their jobs are far more valuable than any amount of money they will earn because they learn the heady lesson of independence ("I can do it! I earned this money myself, nobody handed it to me, and I can do what I want with it.").

Yes, they can do what they want with their money...within your reasonable limits! If Johnny earns the cost of a cat, but his sister sneezes just watching the Persian cross the street, then Johnny has a nonnegotiable restriction on his spending.

Please, may I digress here briefly for a glance at the future? When children reach high school, their earning capacity increases and this increased independence can go to their heads. This particular space is often already filled to capacity with math, languages, science, etc., and any additional load will short-circuit their system. In this book we are focusing our attention on pre-senior high school students, but I want to at least mention the possible negative effect a real world job can have on a child's scholastic success.

Actually, there are many recent studies from high schools throughout the United States which indicate the short-circuit is not an unusual connection. More and more teachers are reporting that their students sleep in class so they can be bright-eyed on the job. These youngsters are not so much early addicts to workaholism as they are addicted to consumerism. A new VCR is a lot more fun than a math class, even if you have to flip burgers to buy it. Had these older students been exposed to your financial education when they were young, I very much doubt they would fall for the lure of short-term job rewards when a long-term success is clearly available to them.

Before I took that brief detour into the high schools, I was talking about the values your children receive from their introductory job experiences with you. In addition to their expanded independence and their heightened self-esteem, your children's pride in their accomplishments is enhanced through the external validation of earned income. They learn to take control of their time and their activities. Their self-confidence builds with their successes at home and they have the courage to try the greater job market, which may well be no further away than next door.

Starting work for pay outside the home

What direction should a child assume when she is ready to leave the safe jobs at home and take on risky business elsewhere? Before I give you some suggestions, let me tell you about a young boy who cut the grass at his own house and then realized there was more of that green stuff everywhere.

Tom cut the lawn every Saturday morning. One day a neighbor asked if Tom would cut his grass in the afternoon. In a few weeks, Tom had six lawns to cut right in his neighborhood. He saved all his money and bought the best lawn mower he could find, rigged up an old wagon so he could pull the mower behind his bike, and soon had some cutting jobs several blocks away. The next summer, Tom had two mowers and hired a friend to help him. It wasn't long before Tom was a familiar figure in town, organizing workers at his house on Saturday morning before sending them off to the jobs he had lined up during the week. When he was old enough to drive, his father helped him buy a used truck. Then Tom drove around town after school, weekends, and all summer long, dropping off his workers with their yard equipment, picking them up, and calling on his accounts to collect the checks. One truck led to another and to another; by the time Tom graduated from high school he had a thriving lawn and garden business. He went to college at night and eventually received his degree, which he hung on the office wall at his company's headquarters.

Tom's experience would please Voltaire who believed that "work spares us from three great evils: boredom, vice, and want." Or, as Albert Camus expressed it: "Without work, all life goes rotten."

Well, we don't want our kids to have rotten lives, so what can we suggest they do to avoid it? They can baby-sit, dog- or cat-sit, take care of the neighbors' plants, be a party helper or a mother's helper, run a summer play school, tutor younger children, hold a used toy sale, work on a farm, pick fruit, have a paper route, do errands for older people, do yard work, give music lessons, plus all the jobs they did at home when they worked for you.

Importance of work habits and skills learned at home

Your children are the fortunate ones when they look beyond home for their jobs. You have already given them good work habits and taught them a variety of job skills. Still, when they work for others there are some added concerns. For example, help your child realistically assess her abilities. If she decides to give a puppet show and charge admission, she had better know how to make a puppet dance or there will be no repeat performance. If your child decides to baby-sit, she should be prepared for all the responsibilities this job requires. You can send for a free guide called *The Super Sitter*, by writing to the U.S. Consumer Product Safety Commission, Washington, DC 20207.

But even the best skills and most clever ideas won't earn money unless there is a customer eager to pay. Children need help in finding ways to get a job. Most neighborhoods have bulletin boards at drugstores, the library, grocery stores, or on community kiosks. Your child, with some advice, can design a business card or a flyer to post in these locations and also leave at neighborhood houses. Many churches and synagogues allow young people to advertise on a "youth available" bulletin board. If none of these efforts produces customers, then it is time to reassess the particular service or skill your child is selling. She can distribute a questionnaire asking: "Do you have any jobs I can do for you?" Her name, age, past experience, and phone number (with contact hours) can be printed on this flyer.

A cautionary note

Note: In every instance where children advertise job skills, parents must first evaluate any possible invasion of privacy or potentially unwelcome attention resulting from public disclosures of information regarding their children. Children must never work for anyone without first receiving advance parental permission. The primary consideration is your children's safety!

If your child decides, for instance, to find a job as a party helper and advertises without success, will she be crushed? I think so, but you can turn her defeat into a major victory. Let her know that the lack of customers has nothing to do with her or her ability, but rather is a reflection of consumer demand. Offer alternative job suggestions; provide all the help you can to assure her a success. Then she learns the painful but wonderful sequence of rejection, perseverance, and triumph! She won't be afraid, in other words, to take a risk in the future. She won't give up when her first try at a job does not produce results. This is a child who has the courage to fail — one of the most potent ways to reach any goal.

Fortunately, children who have a skill or service to sell and are willing to work hard and well rarely lack an opportunity to earn money. Would you consider a broken string on a tennis racket a major opportunity? I certainly didn't until I heard the story and saw the success. Ann Landers, who is wiser than I, would not have required any proof. She is credited with the observation: "Opportunities are usually disguised as hard work, so most people don't recognize them." Andy did.

Andy is twelve and he has his own business cards, his own telephone in his "home office," and his original debt to his father (twelve hundred dollars) is almost paid off. His company, Strings, Inc., started when he found out how expensive it was to have the broken strings repaired on his own tennis racket. His father taught him how to do the repairs himself. Soon Andy's friends were coming to him for repair jobs on their rackets. He decided to buy equipment, set up a workshop, and go into business.

Money earned is money valued

This success story is just one of the hundred I have heard when children told me how they earned money. I agree Andy's story is particularly dramatic, but he has learned no more or less than his counterparts. All of these working children, whether they earn two dollars picking weeds, ten dollars baby-sitting, or an occasional few dollars at any job, know what it means to take responsibility and be accountable for their actions. They are meeting adults other than their parents or teachers in situations where they discover that not all adults have the same opinions, attitudes, standards, or behavior. They may find out there are adults who care more about the job than who is doing it; their egos are enhanced but these children do not become egocentric. They learn the difference, sometimes, between humanity and inhumanity; when their feelings are hurt, they become more sensitive to the feelings of others. Certainly they are more considerate as consumers when they have had a chance to be a producer or seller. And as Gloria Vanderbilt once remarked in a television interview, "The only money I ever valued was the money I earned."

When a child translates the cost of a tape deck into the number of cars she washed to pay for it, that item assumes a value not represented solely by the price tag. When baby-sitting money buys designer jeans, those are not the pants your child will wear on a camping trip. I believe all recreational activities have heightened enjoyment when a child earns the price of admission.

Learn today — earn tomorrow

Children have this wonderful capacity to learn and to earn while they are still shielded by the non-threatening environment of home. When we give them skills and self-esteem, they can meet any challenge in the future. Our society is in transition; we are moving from a manufacturing economy to one dominated by service industries and information providers. There is no way we can prepare our children for a specific job — that job may be obsolete by the time they fill out the application or send in a resume. But the attitudes your children acquire — both toward work and toward their ability to perform it — will allow them to be successfully competitive in any environment.

When I use the word "competitive," I do not necessarily equate it with the singular goal of money. Some of the most satisfying work for children (and adults) would best be described as a project, and is sustained by inspiration, dedication, and creativity, not solely by the profit motive.

One summer the neighborhood "gang" — a band of six children, the youngest only four and the oldest well into his ninth year — were bored with free time and wanted to trade their play for pay. One mother of this ambitious group suggested they go into the newspaper business. A typewriter, a dictionary, pencils, and a basement became the hub from which flowed the weekly edition of *The Grasshopper*.

Scott was elected publisher (a designation awarded for his advanced years). Betsy, the four-year-old, was cub reporter, pencil sharpener, and contributed the most when she went home to take her nap. Three mothers were involved by birthright and took turns as consultants for such crucial matters as liability, freedom of the press, editing debates, and equal distribution of lemonade and cookies.

The children interviewed neighbors for lead stories: Mrs. Walters has a sick cat; Suzie Dalton visited her grandparents in Missouri; Mr. Jenkins bought a new car; Jackie Davis lost a tooth. To meet expenses (and with luck, make profits) they sold subscriptions and solicited ads from local businesses. They also took paid ads in their "job wanted" column. *The Grasshopper* reporters covered the territory; local events, rotary meetings, and political campaigns — their notebooks were open at all times to capture the life in their community. The paper ran a city government column, a want ads section, news of real estate transactions, a "this week's birthday" notice, and accepted all hot tips from credible sources. During the three years of publication, one highlight was a feature story in the major competitor's paper (the city daily) that included pictures of the entire *Grasshopper* staff and a lengthy write-up of their activities. By the time the paper folded (attrition wiped out the staff), the neighborhood "gang" was ready to take on the world.

Did a kids' newspaper pay off?

Was the hard work, for both the children and their parents, worth the effort? Did the job pay off?

The paper met expenses. Actually, it turned a profit — but this was regularly consumed by growing appetites. The most reliable evaluation comes from the staff of *The Grasshopper*. You can find them today in a law office, behind the desk of a corporate headquarters, in a college classroom, and on the masthead of a popular publication.

5.
All that
Glitters

There was a time when parents, grandparents, and an occasional aunt or uncle were the only ones who never tired of focusing attention on "their" child. Now this devotion flows unabated from total strangers dedicated to your child's pleasure, who want him to have nothing but the best and the most that life — and they — can offer. These strangers are known as marketers.

If, through some peculiar circumstances, your child fails to recognize what is best for him, or if by some quirk he is satisfied with what he has, then the marketers put their heads together (or else their heads will roll) to plan new advertising campaigns to stimulate your child's acquisitive consumer instincts.

How can we prove to our children that Madison Avenue is not an exclusive residential area occupied by fairy godmothers? Oh, my; providing the proof is a formidable task. For one thing, reality has less glamor than fantasy. For another, Madison Avenue has an endless supply of those little magic wands they wave at children who sit in front of TV sets, look at magazines, or wander through the aisles of stores and shops. Face it: the odds are against us!

Advertisers work with budgets that would let any of us retire in luxury. Their promotion efforts don't suffer the distractions we encounter such as loose teeth, buttons, and pets. They have access to the media, while we have only intelligence and common sense at our command. (It is estimated that children see twenty thousand TV commercials each week.)

Against these overwhelming odds there is, it seems to me, only one successful course we can take: "If you can't beat 'em, join 'em." Teach your children to be smarter, better, more shrewd, and more clever in the field of creative advertising and marketing than any of the professional players.

In a field crowded with products designed to capture your child's attention and his money (not to mention yours) it borders on unfair to pick one as an example, but we must start some place. Let's begin with food. Specifically, let's take a look at cereal.

Product testing can be fun...and educational

Imagine a cereal producer who wants children to demand "Spiffies" for breakfast every morning. Before he puts Spiffies on the supermarket shelf, he hires an advertising agency to create a demand for his product. Assume the promotion is effective and your child announces: "I won't eat Brand X. I want Spiffies."

Here is your opportunity to put your child in charge of product testing, cost analysis, and promotion effectiveness. In spite of the big words, children of all ages can become experts. In fact, children love the challenge once they find out how to meet it.

Greet your child's demand for Spiffies with all the curiosity you can muster toward a new cereal. Enthusiastically suggest: "Yes, the next time we go shopping, let's look for Spiffies. Let's find out why this cereal is so much better than all the others. Do you think it will cost less or more than the cereals we buy now? Will it taste as good as your Brand X?"

On the next shopping trip, take along a pencil and paper. Plan to spend extra time in the cereal section so you can show your child how to compare the prices in terms of weight and content, not just by box price alone. Pick several cereals for your comparison study and write down the brand names, cost, and some basic information about the nutritional content. Ask your child to describe why one box has greater appeal than another — is it the color, the pictures? What makes him like the appearance of the cereal? Let your child select five different kinds of cereal to take home and submit to actual taste testing. Make a game of this! Explain that a taste test has no value if the tasters know what they are eating. Pour a few bites of each cereal into separate bowls. If your child doesn't mind the feel of a blindfold, let him play the game without seeing the shapes and colors of the products. Otherwise, shift the test bowls around and don't let your child know which brand he is tasting. Keep a scorecard to mark down his responses. For example, Bowl #1 may taste "awful," "funny," "good," "super." When he finishes the cereal tasting, let him see how he rated and compared the products. If Spiffies wins the taste test, price test, and content analysis, then maybe the producer has a new product you should buy. If Brand X wins in every category, then it's time to let your child tell you what he has learned about advertising. Help him ask questions about the techniques advertisers use to sell a product. Did the Spiffies live up to all the promises made about it? What was the one fact, picture, cartoon, and so on that made him want to eat the cereal? If Spiffies cost more, is it worth the money? Why?

Kids can learn comparison shopping, too

Once your child masters the cereal shelves, let him experiment with other food products. Even if you don't always buy an assortment of brands, have your child do comparison pricing while he shops with you. For example, one mother I know puts her children in charge of fresh produce. They keep a weekly list of the prices on fruits and vegetables and let her know when the best time is to buy lettuce, melons, green peppers, etc. Another parent has her children collect all the savings or bonus coupons for products the family buys on a regular basis; when they go grocery shopping, the children can pocket all the money they save from the usual food bill. She says this is a real incentive for her children to be better shoppers and makes them aware of how much it costs to feed a family. I see benefits from all these activities: the children learn to spell new words (zucchini?), they practice their arithmetic (29 cents a pound, or a five-pound bag for $1.39?), and they have something constructive to do while you do the shopping.

A few weeks ago, while pushing my shopping cart down the aisle of a supermarket, I saw a boy writing down brand names and prices for packages of snack foods: pretzels, cheese crisps, potato chips, and so on. I thought, "Oh, terrific! Here is a child actually comparison shopping." I introduced myself, explained why I was interested in what he was doing, and asked him if he was making a study for a school project. "No," he said, "my family has an export business and I'm checking on products we will market in Hong Kong." Admittedly, I was a bit flustered to meet a sophisticated international food marketer engaged in product research who was, he told me, thirteen! Yes, something constructive to do...while I am only shopping.

Learning from TV commercials

When you watch television with your children, focus their attention on the commercials. I know this isn't your greatest pleasure in life, but we are competing with professionals. And actually, when children are told to watch commercials and while watching them they are asked to analyze their purpose and effectiveness, they become shrewd observers and a discriminating audience for Madison Avenue's best and brightest. Be fair, though; if an ad is very good, give it credit, and if a product lives up to the promises, the producer deserves recognition.

While we are still on the subject of food, I want to quote one of the parents I interviewed. "My daughter is in the sixth grade and has just completed her third nutrition class in about the same number of years. She now knows everything there is to know about protein, carbohydrates, and fiber, but she knows absolutely nothing about what food costs. Why are the schools overemphasizing nutrition while totally ignoring the economics that teach children how to buy this healthy food?"

As the talk show guests wisely respond, "'That's a good question." For this parent, the answer is not all bad. Many schools are teaching economics and some of these courses are excellent. As of 1986, forty states had included into the required public school curricula some form of instruction in consumer economics. There are programs available for every class level, first grade through high school, and if your school district does not currently have a consumer education program, you may want to encourage your local district to include one.

Consumer education programs in grade school

Kinder-Economy (primary grades) and Mini-Society (intermediate levels) are two examples of proven success. Both of these programs were created by Marilyn Kourilsky, director of teacher education at the UCLA graduate school of education. The schools in Kansas City, Missouri, have an ambitious consumer education program called The Learning Exchange in which fifth and sixth graders play-act the functions of consumers, producers, bankers, job seekers, employers, etc. Following an intensive course in the classrooms, the children practice their new skills in a simulated town, Exchange City, located near the downtown area.

No school, regardless of the quality of a particular course it may offer, can provide the quantity of consumer information children need if they are to cope with the complexities of our consumer-oriented society. Audrey Guthrie, quoted earlier in this book, believes there is more to consumer education than facts and figures. As she expresses it, "Children can learn the mechanics of check writing, but how they use the money is set by the parents." Professor Guthrie speaks to the central issue from which all other aspects of consumerism take their directions: values. In this sense of the word, values are not the quality or the market price of products, but rather, they reflect the significance a consumer attaches to the product.

Are clothing labels all-important?

As an illustration, let's look at the significance of the various labels attached to the apparel market. The statistics on the consumer dollars spent in this market range between fourteen and thirty billion dollars each year. The lower figure reflects money spent on children's (ages four to twelve) clothing; the higher figure is an estimate of the teen market. Somewhere in this multi-billion dollar market there are blue jeans for sale. When your child pulls on a pair of this American tradition, which is most important for him: the cost, the fit, or the label?

According to the children in my survey, the most important

feature of jeans is the label. They did not say so, but for some children a designer label makes them feel "upwardly mobile," and this direction has greater significance than their ability to bend over and touch their toes. Not surprisingly, parents place the greatest emphasis on cost and fit; designer labels deserve the hindmost attention. Here is a clash of consumer values and (unless the parents are intimidated) a potential clash between parents and children. Clearly, the influences of advertising and peer pressure are so powerful they cannot be ameliorated by reason or persuasion. If you are to maintain your parental values, you must use a compromise solution rather than the test market system so effective in selecting food, as illustrated in the Spiffies example, and in buying toys or games (which we will explore later). Almost without exception, the parents I interviewed use a compromise similar to this one described to me by the father of a fourth grader.

A compromise that worked

"Linda needed new jeans and we were all set to buy them for her when she told us they would cost forty-eight dollars. We hit the roof! No way were we going to shell out fifty bucks for a pair of pants she would outgrow in a few months. Her mother and I told her we didn't care what the other kids wore, we weren't about to become victims of advertising and trendy fashions. (And when jeans fade, can other trends be far behind?) Of course, nothing we said made any difference — she told us all her friends wore jeans and if she didn't, kids would think she was weird. Finally, I came up with a solution. I told her we would give her the money for a regular pair of jeans and if she wanted the designer ones, she would have to pay the difference out of her own money."

"Did she buy the designer jeans?" I asked.

"Oh, sure, but it was interesting to watch her shop for them. I bet she went to six different stores checking on prices before she spent her money. She never does that when we are paying. We think we're onto something — maybe we'll do this for all her clothes."

Perhaps Linda, too, as her father puts it, "is onto something." As a comparison shopper, she is learning about monetary values;

when she must use her own money for the labels that add to the cost of the basic clothes her parents pay for, she is also learning the significance of her parents' values concerning clothing. It is much easier to resist peer pressure and advertising when your consumer instincts are governed by your own wallet. Sometimes the resistance becomes so effortless there are situations when parents have to drag their children into stores and beg them to buy things — even when the parents are paying the bills! At the age of twelve, Tracy, for example, already has formed her non-spending habits.

Tracy is one of three children in a most affluent family. She receives an allowance and earns additional money by baby-sitting. I asked her what she did with her money.

"Mostly, I save my money. I'm just not a shopper. I belong to Campfire and when I needed a uniform, I bought a hand-me-down. My friends buy a lot of candy and posters (they cost two dollars each!), but I think that's a real waste of money. When I see something good that I really want I'll have enough money saved so I can buy it."

Tracy's mother told me: "I can't get her into a store. She always tells me she has all the clothes she needs. Last year I tried to talk her into buying a new coat but she said, 'Why? The one I have still fits me.' Maybe we have taught her too well that money should not be wasted."

Tracy's mother was being facetious, of course, and I could tell she is proud that her child, though raised in a wealthy environment, is not inclined to squander money. At the end of our conversation she said, "It's so much easier to give things to our children than to teach them the value of money, but we can't predict their futures, and we won't always be around to take care of them, so we feel we must teach them how to manage for themselves."

I'm sure we would all agree it is easier simply to provide for our children within our financial limitations, and many parents follow this less complicated route. But they also worry about it, as I discovered when I listened to this physician's story.

"How is the new book coming along?" he asked me.

"Slowly," I replied. "It takes a long time to interview so many children and parents. Maybe I should interview you — how old are your children?"

"We have two girls, ten and twelve, and I worry about their attitudes toward money," he said. "I grew up in a poor family and my parents didn't wonder whether or not we had too much too soon. If all you can do is manage the basics, the essentials, you have no reason to ponder the luxuries."

"Do you think your daughters have a healthy respect for money?"

"No, they don't. The oldest likes to baby-sit; last week she brought me her money and asked if maybe she should do something with it. There was almost two hundred dollars! She had been shoving one- and five-dollar bills into her bureau drawer for months."

"Doesn't she ever want to spend her money?"

"I'm afraid she doesn't have much opportunity. For example, my wife and I gave the girls their own telephone last year; I know we should insist they pay at least part of that bill, but..." he hesitated, "that takes time. It's easier for us just to pay for things."

Taking the time to teach values

He is so right: it does take time to teach children how to spend money. In traditional families where one parent earns the money and the other is home all day, there is greater opportunity to teach children consumer values, both the functional and ethical. However, there are over sixteen million women who are working mothers with children under the age of thirteen. In these households there is barely enough time to do the shopping, let alone find the time to teach young children how to do it. But children learn by example, and while you may not intend to teach your children a lesson in consumer economics, they are learning every time they see you buy something or hear you discuss your spending.

Children don't have to be passive consumers

Whether or not you are an in-home parent, you may want some outside help in teaching your children how to be expert consumers. For $11.95 a year (this makes a great gift for kids) you can subscribe to the consumer magazine *Penny Power* (Penny

Power, P.O. Box 2878, Boulder, CO 80322). In addition to games, puzzles, stories, and articles all dealing with consumer issues, this first-rate magazine regularly features test marketing surveys for products children want to buy. But since *Penny Power* can serve only as a supplement to your own instruction, you are still the main source for helping your children to evaluate the things they desire, such as toys, games, skates, bikes, tennis rackets, etc. Despite thoroughly evaluating a product before you buy it, there will be occasions when an item fails to meet your expectations. It could be a toy that breaks or falls apart soon after you bring it home, a shirt that shrinks, or a game that does not live up to the features advertised by the manufacturer. Show your child he does not have to be a passive consumer. Some items can be returned to a retailer, some carry a warranty or guarantee, others can be exchanged for a credit voucher. In any instance where the reality of a product falls short of your reasonable expectations, help your child write a letter to the manufacturer (preferably addressing it to the president of the company). Be very specific when you draft your complaint and include information as to where you purchased the item, how much you paid for it, and how long you have owned it. If you bought the item as a result of advertising, send a similar letter to the television station, magazine, or newspaper that ran the ad.

CARU: an information source for young consumers

All advertising directed at children under the age of twelve is reviewed and evaluated by the Children's Advertising Review Unit of the National Advertising Division, Council of Better Business Bureaus. (Whew! A name as long as a commercial.) CARU is a source of information for children, parents, and educators concerned with the integrity of advertising, particularly when it misleads children or makes deceptive claims. CARU's guidelines are expressed in five basic principles; it is interesting to note that the final principle states: "It remains the prime responsibility of the parents to provide guidance for children." None of us will argue with that! When you study the detailed list of guidelines for advertising directed at young children and at the same time watch TV commercials on a Saturday morning, you understand why CARU includes an admonition for parents to take responsibility.

Consumers have a right to make legitimate complaints, and contrary to one school of thought, manufacturers want to hear about flaws in their products or negative responses to their advertising. They are in business to make money by selling, and it is an odd company indeed that deliberately seeks failure by disappointing the consumers. An added benefit of writing is that when your child receives his response from the manufacturer, he also gains insight into his direct relationship with the world of commerce.

...and how to make choices

Before your child selects any product, show him how to analyze it from several angles. Will it give lasting pleasure, or is it an impulse purchase based on advertising? How will it be used? If it is a game, with whom will he share it? If it is a toy, go to the store and examine it for durability, and also evaluate how suitable it is for his age and environment. I am reminded of the time I lived in an apartment and the children upstairs practiced roller skating on the kitchen floor, or the time parents in another apartment gave their child a battery-operated toy that tooted and whistled at me every time (or so it seemed) I sat down at my typewriter. Most definitely, no child who aspires to fame as the drummer in a rock band should live within miles of the nearest neighbor!

Among the realities that contribute to becoming an astute consumer, there is a basic truth that can elude even the most proficient shopper: one must make choices. No, Virginia, there is no fairy godmother.

When children are bombarded with the message "More is better and most is best," it requires some ingenuity on our part to demonstrate the finality in that rare word ENOUGH! I am grateful to the many parents who taught me their creative methods for making children aware that life is a selective process, not an indiscriminate grab-bag event.

Leonard, a salesman and father of two, related the following story. "I discovered 'pay as you go' after several vacations where I spent a good deal of time making all the decisions for my kids. 'Can I have a soft drink?' 'Can I buy a magazine?' 'How about these postcards?' 'I need film.' And on and on. I was tired of saying yes, no, maybe, we'll see. Now when we take a trip, each boy gets about thirty dollars for the week. They have to pay for between-meal snacks, small gifts to take home for relatives or friends, video arcades, movies, and souvenirs. I usually buy each of them one gift from the trip, maybe a T-shirt or a game. They know to the penny what they have spent, where they spent it, and how much they have left to spread over the rest of the trip. I started the 'pay as you go' system when the boys were eight and ten. At first I worried they would lose their money, but when it's all they have, they really hang on to it. I'm surprised at how well they budget and how generous they are — no matter how small, they always find something to take to friends back home."

Sharing the planning for special events

Maureen, a secretary and mother of three, told me her approach: "I don't keep my children on a strict budget, but I do let them know we have just so much money for extra things like movies, meals in restaurants, a day in the city, or a trip to the mountains. I can only afford one of these special events a month, so I let the children take turns picking out what we will do. We all plan how much money will be spent on that special outing and I pay for all of it because it's a family event. For instance, if it's Jill's turn to pick our special day together, she gets to plan what we do but has to stay within the budget we set for it. A day in the city will cost us maybe fifty dollars, but a movie would only be twenty with popcorn and an ice cream on the way home. It works out to be fair, though, because they take turns and help decide on the amount we can spend."

Beth, a nurse and mother of two, relates: "It seems that no sooner do I pay the bills for the new school clothes than I start hearing about all the things my kids want for Christmas. One method that works well for me is to take the girls on a pre-holiday shopping trip. When they were real little, I would write down all the things they wanted, along with the prices. Now they keep their own 'wish lists,' also including the name of the store where they saw something and the name of the manufacturer. This is a great help for their grandparents, who never know what to send them or where to buy it. Our 'choose but don't buy' trips can get pretty frantic. 'Come look at this, Mommy.' 'That's what I want this year.' 'You gotta see this, Mom.' When the girls have something specific to do like making their own lists, it ends most of the begging, pleading, and nagging I used to hear before holidays and birthdays. They know they won't get everything on their lists, but this lets them have some dreams, and we all need a little of that in life. When they get home, they arrange their lists in order of importance (and believe me, that changes constantly). Also, when they have the prices on their lists, they can see just how expensive dreams are. As we get closer to Christmas, they revise, add, and subtract from their lists, and make decisions about the items that are really important to them and the ones that were just whims. I think children should make decisions so they don't feel like powerless little people no one listens to. And it's awfully nice for me to hear, on Christmas morning, 'Oh, boy, that's just what I wanted most.'"

Sam, an insurance agent and father of one, told me: "Whenever I take my son shopping with me I always remind him to bring his own money in case he sees something he wants. You would be amazed at how tight he is with his own money. Besides, I avoid a lot of controversy this way because I don't have to say 'no, you can't have that.'"

When is a child old enough to learn?

As you read how other parents find ways to help their children make choices, you may wonder at what age your child can grasp this vital concept of consumer economics.

Uncle Ed took his sister's family out for Sunday brunch. On the way to the restaurant, he told the three children he would stop at a discount toy store afterwards and he had a new five-dollar bill for each of them to spend on anything they wanted. While they waited to give their orders, the four-year-old said, "Uncle Ed, the toy I want costs ten dollars. Can I get it?"

"No, Sarah, I told you I would give you five dollars, and that's it."

She thought about this for a second and said, "What if I don't eat very much? Can I have the extra money for my toy?"

Jokingly her uncle replied, "If you don't eat anything, I'll give you the cost of your brunch."

"Well," said Sarah, "I wish you had told me about this before we left the house — I would have had something to eat at home."

Perhaps we could arrange for Sarah to take a leave of absence from kindergarten so she can go to Washington as a consultant for government spending programs!

Unlike Sarah, many children don't know how much money it costs to buy meals or toys (or anything else, for that matter) because they never see or touch dollar bills. They only know little squares of plastic, and they only hear, "I'm going to get that — I have VISA." You might as well teach your children there is a fairy, her name is VISA, and she hands out little plastic wands. Do you want a new bike? VISA will get one for you. Would you like a radio, a television set, how about some skis, or ice skates? Ah, VISA is here. I don't mean to single out one brand of plastic card, but MasterCard sounds like an obnoxious little boy in a British novel.

Learning the value of money in a credit card society

Increasingly we transact all our consumer affairs without money; the cashless society. Before the advent of charge cards parents worried that their children would think all purchases were exchanged for a piece of paper on which you wrote some numbers and your name. Today we have both checks and charge cards, but tomorrow both may become obsolete as we punch our consumer identification numbers into telephones and computers. We must keep our children in touch (and I do mean touch!) with the reality that behind all the symbols lurks the genuine article: currency.

Paying with cash...

Practical demonstrations of this reality will cost you a minor inconvenience, but will save your child from a future of self-inflicted financial abuse in the form of debt and interest payments. Spend money! Go to your bank and obtain cash for a week's purchases of food, gas, clothes, recreation, etc. Let your child count the amounts it takes to buy things and let him hand real money to retailers and service providers. Pay cash for dinner in a restaurant, show your child the bill, the tax added to the cost of the meals, and teach him how to figure out the correct tip. Remind your child of the value of money by offering him comparisons in terms that have meaning for him. For example, if your child wants a radio that costs thirty dollars and also wants to go places in the family car, draw his attention to how much it actually costs to fill an empty gas tank and add a quart of oil. Let him see that financial decisions must be based on choices — in this instance, it could be the difference between a radio or transportation.

...and with credit cards

For one month, save all your copies of the customer receipts from credit card purchases. When your charge statement arrives at the end of the month, sit down with your child and show him how each receipt is recorded on the statement, point out the total of all the charges, and give him a specific example of the additional cost incurred when one pays interest. For instance, if your statement totals four hundred dollars, and you have only enough money to pay one hundred, you will owe extra money next month because you have a debt of three hundred dollars. If the interest rate is ten percent, there is that thirty dollar radio the child wanted — headed for the bank, not his bedroom.

You cannot blame children for thinking a credit card allows them to buy something without paying for it; they never see money exchanged for goods or services. We must translate plastic into dollars for our children or we will be guilty of adding their names to the list of irresponsible consumers who believe they can have it all, they can have it now, and they will have it forever.

6.
Saving
Graces

Save time, energy, space, natural resources, an endangered species. Save money? You must be kidding!

Always there is a segment of our population eager to embrace a plan for saving anything other than money. Add a dollar sign to the plan and save becomes an abhorrent word of four letters. The result is a nation with the highest consumer debt and with a national debt that boggles my calculator. Americans have turned indebtedness into an art form; politicians use excessive (and deficit!) spending as a platform. If we want our children to shun this precedent of debt, we must give them attractive alternatives that prove saving money is not a masochistic scheme but is actually the route to unencumbered rewards.

Trust me. You will not convince your youngsters to conserve money by forecasting the weather. No child is impressed with the rainy day philosophy because he knows sunny days bring the best of times: a picnic, a day at the beach, the zoo, a fishing trip.

When you consider how hard it is for us to stash away today's dollars in case we need them for some vague purpose in the future, think how impossible it is for children to save for something they can't identify. Saving for college before you are old enough to drink a cup of coffee is as stimulating as a down payment on a burial plot the day you receive your bachelor's degree. Furthermore, children understand that one of the jobs parents have is to provide full coverage insurance for all rainy days. This is a privilege that goes with the circumstances of childhood.

Nor will you instill in your children the habit of creative saving with forced injections of your authority. ("You will save part of your allowance every week. You will save the money you earn."). This may teach your children to obey you (doubtful) but the most probable effect it will have on their attitude toward saving is one of resentment. If, by some miracle, they don't resent your control over their money, they may turn in the opposite direction and become so enamored of accumulated cash that they learn to hoard their money. "The king is in his counting house, counting out his money" — here are the roots of avarice and greed; don't encourage their growth!

Learning to save...by spending

Contradictory as it may sound, children learn how and why to save when they are forced to spend their own money. And the incentive must be real for them or the reward will not merit the effort and minor discomfort of temporary self-denial. Also, the time between saving for a desire and obtaining it must match the child's age; the younger the child, the shorter the saving period. In other words, don't expect a six-year-old to save twenty-five cents a week so she can buy a car when she is sixteen; she will save twenty-five cents to buy a toy car that costs eighty-nine cents. Let's use this example of a toy car to see how we can prove to a child that saving is not only a bearable process, but it is a workable one that lets you have what you want.

Assume your daughter, Lisa, wants a blue plastic sports car more than anything else in the world. The car costs eighty-nine cents and Lisa has an allowance of fifty cents a week. Since you don't want her to give up all her pleasures and feel miserable while she saves her money, suggest she save only half her allowance. To a six-year-old, four weeks is a long, long time to wait for a reward. You can ease her agony of waiting by offering some visual aids: make a savings chart for her bulletin board, mark off the four weeks, and fasten a plastic bag to the chart so Lisa can watch her savings accumulate. She can cross off the weeks one by one as she drops her quarters into the bag. Find a picture of a little blue car to decorate her savings chart. Give her all the visual and tactile help you can to encourage her to stick with her goal. And on the day when the last quarter drops into the bag, go straight to the toy store so she doesn't have to wait another minute before she can spend her savings on the object of her desire.

Isn't that a perfect example of how a little girl learns what it feels like to want something, to save her money to buy it, and to finally know the joy of reaching her goal? I suspect it is too perfect. What would you do if, at the end of the third week, Lisa decides she really doesn't want the car after all but she will take her seventy-five cents and buy a bag of marbles just like the ones Sue received from her grandfather?

The advantages of saved money

I agree with you; I would do and say nothing. Some parents might feel the saving lesson is wasted because Lisa didn't finish it, or because she changed her mind and bought marbles without waiting and saving specifically for them. These parents forget the purpose of the lesson is to let their daughter discover the advantages of saved money. They are not teaching her to be inflexible; to never change her mind or shift her goals. Rather than consider the exercise in saving deteriorated into a useless chart and worthless effort, these parents should congratulate themselves (and their daughter) for the success of the endeavor. The lesson in saving is not ruined; it is enhanced.

Lisa learns it is not a crisis to change her goal when presented with a new opportunity. It's OK to buy marbles instead of a blue car. She recognizes how satisfying it is to have money already saved so she can buy something she wants without having to wait four weeks to get it.

Nobody can have everything

This is a realistic way to learn the value of saving and accomplishes for more than preaching the old adage "save for the sake of saving." Lisa also finds out her parents trust her to make her own decisions and respect her independence in how she uses her money. But the best lesson she learns from her saving plan is that she can't have it all — life is either a blue car or a bag of marbles.

Obviously, no child is aware of these lessons at the conscious level and certainly neither the parent nor the child puts the actions into words. However, the lessons are learned; they will not be forgotten, and someday they could influence the purchase of a real car which may, in fact, turn out to be a secondhand Volkswagen and shares of IBM stock instead of a brand new BMW.

As children get older, their savings change from quarters to dollars and their saving schedule stretches from weeks into months. In spite of these differences, children still need help from their parents if they are going to believe in the advantages and necessity to conserve their money as opposed to giving in to the glossy temptation of instant gratification which temporarily muffles the squeals from a starving piggy bank.

Talk about your plans for saving money. Let your children know your goals and what you are doing to turn a wish into reality. Naturally they will have more interest in your plans for a family vacation (where to go, what it will cost, how long can we afford to stay, how much money we must set aside each month for the vacation, what we will forego now so we can vacation later) than they will in the new water heater or the payment due on an insurance policy. But be sure to let your youngsters know you save for necessities as well as for pleasures, or they will get the notion that "needs" require no planning, and savings are restricted to luxuries.

Support your children's saving plans

Offer your son or daughter practical support for a saving plan, especially if it involves a lot of money. You may, for example, offer to match each dollar Stan saves toward his new skis. Or you may contribute new boots when he accumulates the cost of skis. If Sally is conserving her spending money so she can go to camp, you can join her in the goal by letting her see you put aside a weekly sum for her swimsuit or her tennis racket. Young savers appreciate both the moral and practical support from their parents. In fact, I like some incentives for my own efforts to save, particularly when the amount is considerable and the duration is extensive.

Remember the ant and the grasshopper

Last fall I was invited to join a summer hiking group for three weeks in the Swiss Alps. This meant I had ten months in which to acquire enough money for my transportation, new boots, meals, and lodging. I cut out a picture of the mountains and fastened it to the door of my refrigerator. Every time I thought of food I was reminded of the beautiful Alps and my hamburgers tasted almost as good as steak when I ate them in front of my incentive. Your children can put pictures of their goals on bulletin boards, closet doors, or inside the lid of a lunchbox.

Regardless of your help and your child's determination, you can't expect every saving plan to reach a successful goal. Children and adults are not immune to temptation. If your kids give in and buy a game with the money saved for a day at the county fair, well . . . cover your ears so you won't hear the groans from the hungry piggy. There is no doubt about it: an empty bank teaches a lesson you will never learn from a full one. I am not seriously suggesting this, but you could give your child a copy of Aesop's fable to read — the one about the grasshopper and the ant — on the day he or she stays home from the fair. No, that would be too unkind and insensitive to give your youngster the story on that particular day. But do, however, make it available some other time. You may recall the fable is about the grasshopper who jumped about all summer and had a glorious time, all the while taunting and teasing the foolish ant who methodically stored up his supplies for the coming season. The days grow shorter, the temperature drops, and the grasshopper is out in the cold while the ant spends a cozy, rewarding winter. Aesop's fable makes an impression with a lasting effect and avoids the harsh, nagging lectures. ("I told you so. Aren't you sorry you didn't listen to me?"). And never once does the ant say, "children must learn the rewards of delayed gratification."

The saving habit; never too soon to start

Apparently there are many adults who missed out on this fable when they were growing up. Robert is fifty-one and plans to retire at age sixty-two. "How much money will I need at that time," he asked, "to give me the standard of living I have now?"

"How much money have you set aside already?" I replied, "and what is your present income?"

"I earn forty-five thousand dollars a year and my savings amount to fifty-two hundred. Up 'til now, it's been too hard to save — seems there are always other ways to use my income. Now I suddenly realize I'd better start thinking about my future."

We are not teaching our children to save for an indefinite goal in an undetermined future. However, when they acquire the saving habit while they are growing up, they will not resist saving when they are adults. We can prepare our youngsters to be financial survivors in whatever economic circumstances they encounter during their lifetimes.

Everyone needs a "safekeeping" place

In addition to realistic incentives for saving, children of all ages need some place to keep their money. When accumulated funds are kept in a pocket or a purse not only are they a present temptation for impulsive spending, they are also not safe from loss or theft. You can make or buy your young saver a bank for his cache, and it should be one he can open, for children like to play with their money; touch it, see it, and count it.

The magic of earned interest

As your child matures his savings follow and coins become dollar bills. Now is your chance to let your child discover that old green magic called interest — a magic that eludes the belief, apparently, of many adults who refuse to acknowledge that money can grow when you don't touch it. In an attempt to give you an objective point of view, you should know my prejudice regarding the importance of teaching children the concept of interest: I consider interest the single most valuable financial fact to teach and to learn! An understanding of interest guides every financial decision to an optimum conclusion whether it is a situation for borrowing, spending, investing, or saving.

I realize that statement is as obvious to you as my saying "you can't win at tennis if you don't play with a racket." Therefore, you may doubt my claim that the consequences of interest must be taught, that they are not simply learned the way one learns shoelaces must be tied or they will cause you to trip and fall.

Think, however, of the millions of Americans who pay from twelve percent to eighteen percent interest on their credit card debt and wonder why they can't save money. Think about the consumers who buy furniture on an installment plan, willingly forfeiting those additional dollars that could have been earning them interest. Whenever I think about the losses adults assume because they either ignore or are ignorant of the value of interest, I recall the woman who sat in the front row one evening as I talked about personal finances. Her eyes never strayed, her attention never wandered (speakers always notice these rare souls). After the class, she asked me for advice. "See my purse?" she said, clutching it to her chest. "I have a check for fifty thousand dollars in here and I have been carrying it around with me for two months. I'm afraid to leave it at home because it might get stolen, but I don't understand about banks and savings. What should I do with it?"

The costs of financial illiteracy

No, she is not a stupid woman — she is simply one who never learned why a check should be rushed to the bank so it will begin to earn interest. This woman was financially illiterate. And you cannot judge her actions on the basis of her sex, education, or her age. I also know men, young and old, with MBA degrees, who pay finance charges, leave considerable sums in passbook savings accounts paying five percent interest, and allow checks to accumulate on their desks because they won't take the time to deposit them. Imagine if you will the thousands (millions?) of neglected dollars aimlessly shuffling around town when they could be hard at work earning their owners new cars, vacations, or decent credit ratings.

A simple lesson in simple interest

Here is a little practical exercise you can use to show your primary grade children how a bank makes money, charges interest to a borrower, and pays interest to a lender (depositor). Jane owns a bank. Mary puts ten pennies into the bank. Sue borrows ten pennies. After a few months, Mary gets back twelve pennies. Sue must return fifteen pennies. Jane earns three pennies because she owns the bank. Actually collect the pennies and make a little bank. Let your youngster count out the pennies as they go in and out of the bank. Children have to go through the motions or you cannot get the information through their heads.

I hope you will tolerate a personal account of how I learned, as a child, the value of interest. I consider myself most fortunate to have had a grandfather who, with wisdom and patience, gave me my earliest lessons in the magic of interest. He showed me how I could let my money go to work for me, and how my thinking about interest affects my spending and saving. My first lesson accompanied the bank he gave me. It was a windmill with a money slot in the top; the blades moved when a coin was dropped into the bank. He offered me an exaggerated rate of interest, one that would capture my attention: every time I saved four quarters of my money, he added one of his own. Talk about incentive!

The cost of money spent in terms of interest

When I was older, around eight or nine, every time I took money out of my bank to spend it, he asked me to tell him how much interest (as opposed to capital) I was spending. For example, the price of a game is five dollars, but in terms of interest the game cost me fifty dollars in capital earning ten percent, and my money must work for me an entire year before it earns my game. You'd be surprised at how quickly children grasp this concept and how readily they apply it to their own financial decisions. I fear we greatly underestimate our children's ability to comprehend economics, and I find this odd in a society that shrugs in nonchalant acceptance at children's mastery of science and technology.

"Graduating" from a piggy bank to a real bank

Despite the reality that no real bank pays an interest rate of ten percent on savings, children should graduate from the home bank to one in their community. As in so many of our financial lessons, the action carries a greater value than the relatively small sums used as tools for teaching. In "the good old days," children learned about banks and banking right in their classrooms. A local bank provided school banking; even first graders had deposit books, saving accounts, and usually a class visit to see where their money went after it left the classroom. Those were also the days when parents taught their kids how to drive. Today the lessons (and the values?) are reversed and now parents must show their children there is more to a bank than the vending machine that distributes cash at the push of a few buttons.

Carl Schmidt, president of University National Bank and Trust, Palo Alto, California, frequently visits schools as a consultant or guest resource. Schmidt told me: "I discover some teachers don't understand the rudiments of the banking business. Parents must get involved and not leave it [financial education] to the educational system." He went on to explain that "today banks can't afford to send personnel into the classrooms, and school savings accounts are no longer economically feasible. Parents must teach banking to their kids. Too many parents want to abdicate all responsibility to the schools, but education can't do everything."

Unfortunately, it is not a simple matter to find a bank where your young saver is welcome. Before you take your child and his savings to a bank, use your telephone for some advance shopping. Find out: what is your minimum requirement for opening an account; will the child have his own passbook or do you supply written statements; do you pay interest on this type of account, and if so, how much; does the interest vary depending on the balance; are there restrictions or penalties on deposits and withdrawals; do you charge any fees and what for and how much? Don't forget to investigate your credit union or the savings and loan banks in your area. When your child does open his first savings account, you may find your bank requires a parent to co-sign and act as a partner in the account. Many banks consider any account as a contract; by law, minors are not allowed to enter into a legal contract.

Tell them how banks work and what they do

Once you identify the institution with the greatest advantages for your child, supply a little homework on the basic functions of a bank. Tell him a bank is a business that makes money by borrowing and lending it. When you put your money in a bank, you are giving them the right to use your money, and in return they pay you (interest) for this use (loan). A piggy bank does not earn you interest. While you are in school, your money in a real bank will be working for you, and eventually you will have more money.

Some invaluable money management primers

Older children will, of course, understand more than that first lesson in banking. You can explain to them how to write a check, what happens to a check once it arrives at the bank, how to fill out a deposit slip for a savings account, why it is vital to keep your own records of all monies deposited or withdrawn from an account, and what the purpose is of a safe deposit box. Ask your bank if you can take your child with you into the safe deposit vault; let him watch the process of opening a box and returning it to the vault. (Children love this!) If you want some free teaching materials, write for these three comic books: *The Story of Banks, The Story of Money, The Story of Checks.* They are available from the Federal Reserve Bank of New York, Public Information Department, 33 Liberty Street, New York, NY

10045. While you have a pen handy, also write to Federal Reserve Publication Services, Public Information Materials, Washington, D.C. 20551, and ask them to send you a list of their materials. (After all, you pay for this with your tax dollars; you might as well enjoy an occasional benefit.) Here is something else you may want to write away for — it is excellent and costs only two dollars. Send your check to: Cooperative Extension Service, United States Department of Agriculture (kids or crops; if it grows, I guess the USDA has a stake in it), West Virginia University, Morgantown, WV 26506, and ask them to send you a series of eight pamphlets entitled *Children Learn Money Management*. These are gems!

Taking the mystery out of banking

One of the chief benefits your child receives from his savings account is familiarity with the world of banking. He no longer sees the building on the corner as a house of mystery. In fact, he probably sees his money in much the same way as a youngster named Dick looked at his cash. Dick's grandfather came to visit and the two of them were sent on an errand to the supermarket. As they headed to town, Dick said, "Grandad, go down that street. Now turn at the corner. See that big building over there? That's my bank and my money is in there working for me so I will have more money." Dick was only five years old.

So far the only type of bank savings program I have mentioned is the standard savings account which (as you well know) pays a paltry rate of interest. When your child accumulates more than a few hundred dollars, you will want to consider an alternative with higher rates. If higher interest rates for even your child's small savings are of primary importance, I suggest you consider pooling his funds with yours into a single account. This does, of course, reduce his sense of sole ownership of his savings, but with tact and a full explanation I'm sure you can overcome this disadvantage.

A few excellent state and local programs

In discussing a saving and banking education for your child I have assumed you do not have an aggressive teaching program in your schools or community. My assumption may not be entirely valid because there are areas in which parents receive great support from local professionals. Within the Mississippi Bankers Association, there is an organization called Young Bankers Section and its goal is to educate youngsters in all aspects of banking. Mark Lewis, vice president of the State Bank and Trust Company, Brookhaven, Mississippi, describes their activities: "We go into the schools and assist teachers in presenting the material. PEP, the Personal Economics Program, teaches children how to balance a checkbook, write a check, apply for credit and keep a good credit rating, and understand the function of the Federal Reserve System; in general, what happens to money." Not only does PEP provide information in the classroom, these bankers also put their money where their mouths are: this statewide organization gives a scholarship to a college student in an "effort to encourage top quality students to enter the banking profession." As a final activity following a school program on banking, PEP invites the class to visit a bank for an on-location tour to examine all they have learned. One aspect of this ambitious program is the publication of the instructional material, *How and Why of Banking*. If Mississippi bankers have found time, energy, and resources to provide students in their state with a banking education, is it not also possible for other states to copy this program? Perhaps you can contact your statewide bankers' association and encourage them to put PEP into your schools.

If you live in Denver, Colorado, your children are supremely fortunate for they can take advantage of the first, and to date the only, banking opportunity in the United States that is dedicated to provide financial education and services exclusively for young people. Young Americans Bank, founded in 1987, offers complete banking services: checking and saving accounts, ATM access cards, bank by mail, loans, U.S. saving bonds, photo ID cards/check guarantee, certificates of deposit, etc. The bank also publishes a newsletter, sponsors financial education seminars, contains a "Challenge Corner," where youngsters can watch videos or read books on finance and banking, and distributes free brochures describing practical money management skills. Should anyone question the desire of young people to participate in responsible financial activities, that person need only look at the immediate success of Young Americans Bank. In the first four weeks the bank was open, over two thousand children established accounts. No matter what the age, any child with ten dollars can open a savings account that will pay daily interest. For further information on the services provided by Young Americans Bank, write to: Education Program Coordinator, Young Americans Bank, 250 Steele Street, Denver, CO 80206.

Parents still exert the greatest influence

Regrettably, Young Americans Bank is unique. It is also unfortunate that most states do not have a school saving/banking program like the one in Mississippi. However, regardless of the opportunities available to children in their schools or in the community, it is the parents who exercise the greatest influence. Children who discern the benefits of saving arrive at that conclusion without leaving home.

7.
Future
Returns

Right now, as you read these words, somewhere in your town or city there are young people in their late teens or early twenties who must make decisions about money. What should they do with that part of their income they do not spend on immediate necessities or place in some form of a savings plan for their short-term goals? Most of these beginning wage earners have heard about the financial opportunities attainable by all Americans: stocks, bonds, mutual funds, payroll investment plans, etc. Perhaps only a handful understand the meaning of these investment terms; you can count on your fingers the ones who have actually had experience deciding how and where to invest their money for long-term goals.

Victorian taboo

We teach our children how to earn, save, spend, and share their dollars, yet we handicap them with ignorance about the available methods for putting their money to work as a way to accumulate more dollars, increase their standard of living, and achieve financial security in the future.

There is not one conscientious parent who fails to give his or her children information on physical safety, sexuality, ethics and morals, hygiene and nutrition, manners and behavior. Our goal is to raise children who will have every opportunity to function as physically, mentally, and emotionally healthy adults. Why, then, is it acceptable to send our young people out into the world to flounder, helpless and ill-prepared, in their adult financial situations? Are we looking at the last Victorian taboo: "Nice people don't tell their children where money comes from"? I believe children deserve something better than a "birds and bees" explanation for how people make money.

Knowledge about investing is essential

I am not the only one who considers knowledge about investing money an essential part of a child's basic financial education. There are numerous individuals, nonprofit organizations, educators, and corporations all striving to counter investment ignorance through a variety of creative methods. Though the methods may vary, there is a common conviction in most of these efforts: children should begin their investment education when they are young.

Start teaching the concepts early

Well-known financial planner Ron Murphy defines "young" by suggesting you "talk about your own investment decisions at the dinner table. Children should be exposed to the vocabulary and concepts of investing as soon as possible." He started his own children in an active investment program when they were eight years old. Murphy makes sure his children have jobs in addition to an allowance so they can earn extra money to invest. He prefers a mutual fund for their initial investment experience and helps them locate, in the fund prospectus, the companies held by the fund. "Point out the names of companies with special meaning for your children in their everyday lives," he advises. "Show them the companies that make the food they eat, the clothes they wear, the games they play, and the sports equipment they use." Murphy also recommends all income from invested dollars should be automatically reinvested so children can learn how capital increases to eventually produce greater income. When I asked Murphy what he considers the most important financial fact parents can teach their children, he replied: "Teach them to spend ten percent less than their total net earnings and to put the ten percent into an investment where it will grow."

Alan Lertzman, a vice president of the investment firm Bateman Eichler, Hill Richards says, "Children are like sponges, eager to soak up new information; it is a shame to pass up this time in their lives when they are receptive to ideas about investing." Lertzman became convinced of the need to teach children how to invest as a result of his experiences with adult clients. He cites two typical examples. "One of my clients has made a gift of stocks to each of his children every year since they were born. The oldest child is now fifteen and the children's accounts have grown significantly in value. Recently, during a meeting with this parent, I asked what his children thought about their portfolios. I was astonished to learn that not only did they not ask any questions, but the parents have never explained the investment basics to them. When I asked why, the response was that the children were too young to understand such things as investing in stocks."

Owning just one share of stock can be a learning experience

Another client, a young man of twenty, came to Lertzman in order to begin a regular investment program. "I proceeded to explain the alternatives available, but it didn't take long before I realized he had absolutely no idea what I was talking about. It seems his parents had told him he should invest some of his money, but had never provided him with any investment knowledge." For several years, Lertzman has volunteered his time and expertise in the public schools where he shows children how they can become partners (shareholders) in America's businesses. "Parents can teach their children how to invest by giving them only one share of stock," he says. "Show them how to find their stock in the daily newspaper and teach them how to track the prices of that stock so they can watch the value fluctuate."

Owning one share of stock is obviously not going to turn your child into an instant millionaire, so you do not have to worry that ten-year-old Suzie will face an income tax crisis before you face the crisis of her first date. It is the practical experience of owning stock that serves as the valuable teaching method for your child's financial education. I like the idea of buying children stock in an individual company because they have a direct sense of participation in the investment process. For example, when you buy shares in Minnesota Mining and Manufacturing Co. (3M), they not only send you a letter to welcome you as a shareholder, but they also send you a sample gift package containing an assortment of their products that could include Scotch Tape, Post-it Note Pads, a scrub-sponge, etc. 3M is investor friendly!

Be creative in getting your child involved

If you have a child who likes to cook, you might consider buying him or her shares in a company that produces food. Campbell Soups, for example, sends their stockholders information about new products and recipes so tempting they lure even someone as lazy as me into spending more time in the kitchen. Perhaps you have a child who hates to brush his teeth — buy him a few shares in a company that makes toothpaste. There are all sorts of creative ways to involve your youngsters with companies that are part of their daily lives (or you hope they get the message and begin to use the products).

When my daughter was a little girl her grandfather sent her five shares of the first company to put a communication satellite into orbit. She became interested in space technology because she owned "a piece of the action." A long (very long!) time ago I received as a birthday present five shares of a company I had never heard of: IBM. Through the years my five shares have grown, with stock splits and stock dividends, to the point where I now have an IBM gift that brings many happy returns.

Children who use the very items their money is helping to produce feel intimately involved with our free enterprise system. Also, direct ownership in a company means they will receive a copy of the annual report. Even very young children enjoy the beautiful photography and the bright pictures of a company's products as illustrated in its annual report.

Another individual actively teaching children how to invest is Karen Cutts, an attorney in Los Angeles and the creator of "Funancials," a seminar for children. Cutts explains her dedication to the financial education of children by readily admitting her own former ignorance.

"Soon after I graduated from law school, I received an inheritance. I realized I did not know what a capital gain was, nor did I have any idea how to take care of the money I inherited. Never, in all the years I was in school, did I have a class in the practical aspects of investing and money management."

Investment games with play money can be instructive

Cutts begins her "Fun-ancial" classes with fifth graders. Each child receives one thousand dollars in play money and immediately begins to learn how to buy stocks and bonds. She recommends you begin by having your child identify corporations in your neighborhood: gas stations, restaurants, department stores, and so on. In one of her classes a youngster decided to put thirty-five dollars of his play money into a passbook savings account rather than invest it in a stock. Cutts helped him realize he had earned ninety-six cents from his six months of saving, when he would have earned a sizeable "paper profit" had he invested in one of the class stock selections. (He also could have lost his money!) She pointed out to him, however, "If you had kept all your money in a piggy bank you wouldn't have earned anything."

"I designed Fun-ancials," she said, "not only to teach children how to make their money grow into more money, but also because I believe good investors make good citizens. We live in a global economy and investing opens children's eyes to world economics. Furthermore, what an individual does with his capital affects the future of the United States; investing has a value for the individual and for the nation."

As I mentioned earlier, there also are corporations and non-profit organizations that have help available for those who want their children to grow up with a good knowledge about the sources of income and an understanding of economics. For basic information on stocks and bonds, you can send four dollars to Publications Department, New York Stock Exchange, 11 Wall Street, 18th Floor, New York, NY 10005. Ask them to send you a copy of their guide, *The Investors' Information Kit*. Upon receipt of six dollars the Educational Services Department (17th floor) of the New York Stock Exchange will send: *You and the Investment World*. When you order this publication, also request their free booklet, *Taking Stock in the Future*. Both of these publications are written for children.

Investment clubs for teenagers

The National Association of Investment Clubs, 1515 E. Eleven Mile Road, Royal Oak, MI 48067, has information on how you can establish an investment club for minors. This is a sophisticated activity, suitable only for teenagers who have already learned the basics of investing. If you have access to a computer, there are a number of companies producing software games and activities that meet the interests of children in grades one through twelve.

Computer investment games, too

Wall Street by CE Software (801 73rd Street, Des Moines, IA 50312) has an excellent investing game for up to nine players. Hartley Courseware, Inc. (133 Bridge, P.O. Box 419, Dimondale, MI 48821) has a most basic game for children in grades one through five called "Money! Money!" Sunburst Communications has three fine programs that tie in with the concepts of economics and investing. They are suggested for children in grades six through twelve: "Whatsit Corporation," "Managing Lifestyles," and "Hot Dog Stand." (You can request a catalog by writing to Sunburst Communications, 39 Washington Avenue, Pleasantville, NY 10570-9971.)

"Introducing Economics," (It's Free)

A truly outstanding publication is available free upon request from the Bank and Public Information Center, Federal Reserve Bank of Boston, Boston, MA 02106. Ask them to send you their booklet entitled *Introducing Economics*. It includes, with each concept of the different areas of economics, three practical examples you can use to teach your children how their money affects (and is affected by) the world around them. Frankly, I learned some things I didn't know, and you may find the same is true for you! The section on business organization is of special help in teaching young investors about corporate America and their participation in its growth.

Help for teachers and the PTA/PTO

The following organizations were created primarily to assist teachers in the presentation of economics and finance. I include them here along with their addresses because you may belong to a Parent-Teacher Association and have an opportunity to begin or improve the quantity and quality of the financial-economic education in your school district. I also include these organizations because, in talking with the directors or presidents, I discovered some were not aware that other groups with similar interests exist. Moreover, a few had no idea what materials are available, how to obtain information, or what activities their counterparts are initiating. Perhaps you can put the right hand and the left together to build a complete resource file for your school.

The Foundation for Teaching Economics, 550 Kearny Street, Suite 1000, San Francisco, CA 94108, states its purpose in its catalog: "To foster understanding of the American economic system and the importance of the individual within that system." The foundation seeks to prepare young people to become economically literate voters, wise consumers, and productive citizens. The focus is primarily on economic education in grades seven to ten. Jean Lacey, director of educational programs, tells me the foundation was started in 1975 to put an end to "economic illiteracy." Today that remains its goal, and the Foundation continues to expand its programs in an effort to reach more of our young people before they enter the adult world of confusing financial choices and potentially disastrous decisions.

The National Center for Financial Education, 50 Fremont Street, San Francisco, CA 94105, was founded about three years ago. Their goal is: "Education dedicated to helping people do a better job of spending, saving, investing, insuring, and planning for their financial future." This organization has a separate program called Financial Education 101. In this classroom study guide for high school students, the NCFE lists its aims as: "Learning how to spend money more intelligently, save money with a high interest income, make informed choices on a variety of investment opportunities, and protect financial accumulation."

The Joint Council on Economic Education, established in 1949, is headquartered at 2 Park Avenue, New York, NY 10016. They have affiliates in fifty states and you can write to them for a current *Directory of Affiliated Councils and Centers* to locate the resource nearest your community. Their programs are available for every grade, kindergarten through high school, and their stated purpose is: "To increase the quantity and enhance the quality of economic education in the nation's schools."

A financial newsletter for children...and more

They provide written materials, games, films, and workbooks, and are currently completing a computer base of all economic resources available to educators. A guide to games is sponsored by the Joint Council and compiled by their affiliate at the University of Minnesota. For information write to the Specialized Center for Games and Simulations in Economics, University of Minnesota, 1169 Business Administration Building, 271 Nineteenth Avenue South, Minneapolis, MN 55455. Their guide includes the manufacturer or publisher of a game, the cost, the recommended age level, a brief description of each game, and address for the producers or distributors of these games. Among the over one hundred listings you will find such familiar favorites as "Invest," "Monopoly," "The Stock Market Game," etc. This booklet is an excellent resource for games to give your children so the entire family can have fun learning more about economics, money management, consumer skills, and investing.

Instruction in simple economics must start early

The National Schools Committee for Economic Education (NSCEE) is located at 86 Valley Road, P.O. Box 295, Cos Cob, CT 06807-0295. President John G. Murphy currently heads this thirty-four-year-old organization whose purpose is: "To bring instruction in simple, functional economics to children at the earliest possible age." The NSCEE policy includes teaching the values of our free enterprise system. Dr. Murphy says, "The longer we studied economic education the more we realized it must begin early. It should at least begin in the first grade! When you teach economics in the classroom your goal is similar to teaching health. You are not training children to become doctors by teaching them health and hygiene. Similarly, you are not training children to become economists when you teach them economics. You are teaching them how to live!" Some examples of the materials produced by the NSCEE include *Sara's Business*, a delightful coloring book for first graders. *Buyer, Beware!* is a play for children in grades one through four; *You Choose* is a workbook that includes stories, games, and puzzles to teach children all phases of economics. I particularly like their explanations and activities for young investors in grades three to seven. As a former elementary school teacher, I regret that these and other materials produced by the NSCEE were unknown to me when I stood in front of my classes, for they are exceptional! It is interesting to note that students in sixteen classes, in fourteen states, showed a forty-four percent improvement in their understanding of economic principles and values after using the *You Choose* workbook. I asked Murphy if parents could write to NSCEE for a catalog and then order the materials for their personal use without waiting for their local schools to include them in classroom lessons. Happily, his answer was "Yes!" Also, happily, the costs are minimal, many in the range of from forty-nine cents to three dollars.

The "Stock Market Game" for lucky Boston school children

And look at what the *Boston Globe* is doing! Twice each year they sponsor a ten-week classroom course called the "Stock Market Game." As school children become proficient in the language and actions of investing they select a sample portfolio to enter into a competition which then is evaluated for top performance by the *Boston Globe*. The winning portfolio entitles the entrant to one share of stock in the *Globe's* parent publishing company.

Dr. Paul Tedesco, chairman of the Department of Education at Northeastern University, is a consultant for the *Boston Globe's* young investors program. Dr. Tedesco confirms the growing interest among educators and the private sector in teaching economics to youngsters. He finds, "Teachers are not prepared to teach economics and first we must educate the educators." To accomplish this goal, Tedesco leads frequent workshops for classroom teachers in the Boston area. "When the 'Stock Market Game' is in the classroom," he says, "we often find the parents want to play."

In other cities, too

Boston is not the only city where children have the opportunity to select a simulated portfolio of stocks and possibly win a share of the real thing. Over four hundred thousand students in twenty-seven states participated during 1987 and the numbers are growing. The Securities Industry Association (120 Broadway, 35th floor, New York, NY 10271) is the resource center for the "Stock Market Game," and they assist school districts to implement this investor's training project in cooperation with local chapters of the Center for Economic Education.

Lots of information available for the asking

As you can see, there is no shortage of information for children and their parents in the areas of finance, economics, and investing. All you have to do is send off your requests for materials (many of them are free or require a nominal charge) and then start educating your own children at home. While we cannot expect our schools to do all the teaching in every subject for us, you may be able to persuade your school to include some of the materials I have listed. No matter how fine and thorough a school economics program is, however, the classroom teacher cannot act as an investment advisor for your children. This is your responsibility (and your privilege). Once you have working knowledge of basic investment opportunities, how can you involve your children in the practical skills so they are actual owners of America's businesses? Some suggestions follow, but please remember these suggestions represent my opinions and experience — they are not absolute truths. You or your financial advisors may not agree with the suggestions and naturally, only you can make the final decisions for any investment situation.

Get your child started as an investor

Give your child one or more shares of stock in a company with a steady record of growth and little or no risk. (This will constitute a custodial account under the Uniform Gifts to Minors Act or the Uniform Transfers to Minors Act.) While profit from a capital gain, income from dividends, and all other tax implications can never be totally ignored, this stock purchase is primarily a learning tool for your child; in this instance, tax consequences do not merit consideration. When the stock certificate arrives, let your youngster examine it before you place it in your safe deposit box. (He may want a photocopy for his bulletin board.) Help him to find the stock symbol for his company in either your daily newspaper or in the *Wall Street Journal*. Make a simple chart, marking off bi-monthly squares, where you and your child can fill in the high/low closing prices of his stock. Explain how stock information is listed in the newspaper: the different exchanges (New York, American, NASDAQ, etc.); the high and low prices for the year, week, and the day; the number of shares traded (bought and sold in one day); and how to read the fractions describing the gain or loss for the day or the week. You may wish to add the fractional amounts and their monetary equivalents to your stock tracking chart so your child will have a ready reference. (1/8 = 12 cents; 1/4 = 25 cents; 3/8 = 37 cents; 1/2 = 50 cents; 5/8 = 62 cents; 3/4 = 75 cents; 7/8 = 87 cents.) In addition to your tracking chart, show your child how to keep a record of his stock purchases. You can make record sheets for them, (there are examples at the end of this chapter) or you can buy an inexpensive investment record book at a stationery or office supply store. Tell your child this is kept by all shareholders for every investment they make so that, when the time comes to sell the stock, the owner will know how much his total profit is and how much tax he owes on the profit. Yes, you might as well let your child find out there is a price for success!

Dividend reinvestment plans; an offer you shouldn't refuse

The next step is to decide what to do about the dividends your child's investment will earn. If he owns a company with an automatic dividend reinvestment plan, I think this is an opportunity you cannot afford to disregard. (For a list of companies offering dividend reinvestment plans, send two dollars to: Public Relations Department, Standard and Poor's, 25 Broadway, New York, NY 10004.) On the other hand, if he will receive an actual dividend check, show him how to record the amount and suggest he save his dividends along with some earnings or gift checks so he can buy more shares in the same company, or shares in another one.

Should you live in an area where the headquarters (home office) of a publicly traded corporation is located, you may wish to have your child buy stock in that company. Perhaps he could actually visit "his" company. If this is not possible, at least he will know the building and have a physical image of what his company looks like. Also, community newspapers have more information in their business pages about local companies and your child will have fun spotting articles about his investment. Maybe he can attend a shareholders' annual meeting!

Take your child to a brokerage office

Someday, when your child is on vacation and the stockbrokers are hard at work, take your youngster to visit a local brokerage office so he can watch the ticker tape, and help him to find his stock as it passes by on the tape. Let him see the activity in a brokerage firm, and introduce him to a broker. Children need to see, hear, and touch their investment as much as possible if they are going to feel included in the stock ownership process. You can't just buy them a few shares and consider the financial education a success. Look for ads and commercials that feature your child's corporation, and help him to evaluate the advertising for his company. If he has an opinion, good or bad, about one of the company's products, encourage him to write a letter expressing his views to the president of the corporation.

Investing in mutual funds is instructive, too

If you decide to invest in a mutual fund for your child, it will be a bit harder to make that investment as real for him as an individual stock. However, by following Ron Murphy's advice at the beginning of this chapter, you can accomplish similar goals. A growth mutual fund has the great advantage, of course, of providing your young investor with diversification, thus reducing the risk inherent in most investments. A fund is also professionally managed (you pay for this!) and does not require the investor to make all the decisions about buying and selling a particular stock. Your library will have information about the no-load (no initial service fee) mutual funds and you can write to these various companies for investment qualifications. The management fee for a mutual fund is probably offset by the greater cost of buying only a few shares of any one company as opposed to purchasing a round lot (one hundred shares) of stock.

I have not suggested teaching your child about bonds because I consider the debt concept as one that should be introduced at a later time when he has mastered the vocabulary and skills for stock purchases. Furthermore, I consider growth stocks a far more appropriate investment for children than are bonds or any other type of investment.

Investing is as normal as spending for children who are taught how

When children grow up in an environment where investing money is as normal as spending it, they will not be in awe of their adult financial circumstances. They may not know all the answers for their future decisions, but they will know how to ask the right questions, they will not be intimidated by fast-talking advisors, and they will have a ready skepticism for the get-rich-quick schemes they encounter.

James Tobin, a Yale University professor of economics and recipient of the 1981 Nobel Prize in economics, wrote in the *Wall Street Journal* of July 9, 1986: "The case for economic literacy is obvious. High school graduates will be making economic choices all their lives, as breadwinners, consumers, and as citizens and voters. They will need the capacity for critical [economic] judgment whether or not they go on to college."

Furthermore, any child who invests his or her own money will have a proper regard for the investments of others. Any inherited money, whether it is five hundred dollars or five hundred thousand dollars, will not look like a lottery prize to someone who knows the patience and effort it takes to build an estate.

I recently talked with a man who had, at age twenty-three, received a considerable inheritance from his grandfather. Now in his forties, he told me how sorry he is that he bought an airplane, took flying lessons, went to Europe for six months, and, in his words, "blew the whole damn estate in less than two years." Now he has no capital, no income from investments, and his three children want to go to college. "If only I had learned about investing," he said, "I would have realized you never spend your capital; you only use the income from your invested money for the luxuries in life."

Financial illiteracy: a form of child abuse

His story of a lesson learned too late is not an unusual one. Have you ever listened to radio talk shows where the host gives investment advice to people who phone in their questions? If not, I suggest you do. It is a sad and depressing experience, but one that will convince you your child must not grow up ignorant about investing. These shows confirm the tragedy of men and women from all educational, occupational, and financial situations who are victims of financial illiteracy.

Don't let your child be a victim

I hope you won't be discouraged if all this sounds complicated and time-consuming. You know how dreadful the directions are for the care, use, and repair of a new appliance, yet how easy it all is when you actually begin to put the words into action. Well, the same holds true for my words about an investment program for your children. You can take the suggestions one step at a time, fit them into your schedule, and match them to the child's level of interest. He won't want to do all these things at once! Above all, have fun with investing. Make it a game and your child will never feel like a stranger when he takes his paper walks down Wall Street.

STOCK RECORD

Company Name: _____

Certificate No.: _____

Stock Purchases

Purchase Date	Number Shares	Cert No.	Cost per share	Total taxes & misc.	Total cost	Avg. Cost per share	Sale Date	Total Sale	Net gain/loss

Stock Dividends and Stock Splits

Date	Rate	New Cert. Nos.	Orig. Purchase Date of stock	New Total	No. Shares	New Avg. Cost Per Share

STOCK RECORD

(Simplified Version for Children)

Name of my company _____ Symbol _____

Stock certificate number _____ Exchange _____

Purchase Date	Number of Shares	Cost of Each Share	Total Cost	Date Sold	Total of Sale

Additional Shares

(Source: P=purchased / G=gift / R=reinvested dividends)

Date	Number of Shares	Source (P/G/R)	Cost	New Total No. of Shares	Certificate Numbers

DIVIDEND RECORDS

Company Name: _____

Year	Date	Amount	Date	Amount	Date	Amount	Date	Amount	Year Total

STOCK PRICE TRACK CHART

COMPANY	JAN	FEB	MAR	APR	MAY	JUNE	JULY	AUG	SEPT	OCT	NOV	DEC	HIGH/LOW
1.													
Symbol:													
Exchange:													
2.													
Symbol:													
Exchange:													
3.													
Symbol:													
Exchange:													

8.
Gifts and Giving

As a nation, Americans are unsurpassed in the art of giving. It is our tradition; we are renowned for it throughout the world. Collectively we are unrecognized when it comes to the reciprocal grace of receiving, but that is no surprise. Among other nations, competition for excellence in ways to receive is practiced with intensity, and apparently these nations wish to spare us from disappointment as amateurs in a field crowded with champions.

Fortunately, as individuals we are exposed to both give and take; we meet these situations almost daily in our lives. By definition, children are not born with tradition. They acquire their customs and beliefs through experience and observation, mostly from their parents. Since children are involved with giving and taking even before they are old enough to talk about it, their patterns for these mores are established long before they are teenagers. Take as proof, for example, one five-year-old who visited his great-grandmother confined to bed in a nursing home. Nine members of the family — four generations! — clustered around great-grandmother's bed. Five-year-old Jamie played with a puzzle he found on her bedside table. When it was time to leave, she said, "Jamie, you take that puzzle along with you. I've enjoyed it for quite some time and now I want you to have it." He immediately turned to his mother and whispered, "I can't take her toy — she needs it. What should I do?"

Learning the art of giving and the grace of receiving

Don't we all hope there will be times when our children think of another before they think about themselves? The day I watched Jamie consider his great-grandmother's pleasure (he saw it as a need, and perhaps he chose the better word) before his own desire for the puzzle, I marveled at his unselfishness and his concern for her well-being. Furthermore, (and this astounded me!) he seemed to realize that his refusal of the gift would deny her the pleasure of giving. How can we instill in our children the art of giving and the grace of receiving? When and where do our children find the patterns to follow that will set the directions they take into adulthood?

The answers are obvious and simple. The patterns are formed at a birthday party, under a Christmas tree, across from the first Menorah candle, and in all the uncelebrated events where children have the opportunity to receive something or the privilege to give anything.

I deliberately use the vague terms something and anything because not all gifts are objects wrapped in bright paper or tied with ribbon bows. In fact, as we all know, the most rewarding gifts are time, thought, and effort. Rather than try to list all the many ways you can teach your children how to give and receive as they advance in age, I think some general guidelines and examples serve us best since the methods are the same for each passing year.

When your child has a birthday, let him be an active participant in the plans whether it is cake and ice cream for seven friends or pizza, a movie, and an overnight for a best friend. Help your child to focus on the pleasure he will give his friends. For example, if it is a group party, let your child choose the favors each guest will receive. What games or entertainment will his guests enjoy? If he wants to celebrate with a best friend, does his guest like pizza, or would he prefer to go out for a chicken dinner? Which movie does his guest want to see? In other words, impress upon your birthday child his responsibility as host and his obligation to give his guests the best time he possibly can.

Responding in kind to a thoughtful giver

This removes the singular purpose of a birthday party which too often focuses attention on the gifts received by the birthday child. In families where there are brothers or sisters of similar ages, some parents think their other children should also receive a gift so they won't feel "left out." I consider this an unfortunate custom because it does not prepare children for the real world where they will not always receive just because they are close to someone who does. Indeed, let brothers and sisters share in the excitement and feel special because they can plan a birthday surprise to give. No matter what the age, any child who receives a birthday gift — any gift — should acknowledge it with a written thank you. Parents can do the actual writing for a preschool child but he can print his name on the note, lick the stamp, and mail it himself. I'm reminded of the many times I read the published letters to "Dear Abby" from disappointed and offended writers who tell of presents sent but never acknowledged. This is inexcusable! I recall one letter from her column describing an aunt who had sent a generous birthday check to her niece and found a "thank you" scrawled under the endorsement on the back of the canceled check. (If I were the aunt, I would cancel my niece's next birthday present.) Children should know they are not simply saying thank you for a check or a present, but more important, they are responding to the kindness and thoughtfulness of someone who took the time and the effort to think of them and their pleasure.

A cash gift belongs to the child, just like an allowance

If your children receive money for any occasion, whether it's a crisp new one-dollar bill or a sizeable check, this money is theirs in exactly the same way their allowance belongs to them. You can't fault a child for not saying thank you if he never sees his gift. Several of the children I interviewed for this book told me: "I always get checks from my grandparents for my birthday or Christmas, but my folks say, 'Isn't that nice! Here, give it to me!' And that's the end of the gift. I think the checks go into a savings account, maybe for college or something, but I'm not sure." In a way, this is not fair to the senders, in this instance, grandparents. It may be difficult for them to shop, or they may not be sure of correct sizes, or the latest popular game and toy. If you take the gift of money and "put it in the bank," you cheat the sender out of the pleasure of giving. In fact, I think children should write two notes when they receive money: the first to say thank you for the present, and the second to say thank you, I bought _____ with your gift money. (A generous gift check might buy your child an introduction to investing!) This lets the sender know how much the child appreciates being able to pick out something special for himself and also gives the sender pleasure in the graphic image of what that special something is.

Help your child enjoy the real values of gift giving and receiving

Christmas or Hanukkah bring outstanding opportunities to show children how to give and receive. This is a season when you can deflect the focus on the quantity of the gifts, the price of the gifts, and combat the materialism fostered by advertisers. Some families use the December holidays as a time to prepare gift packages of food and toys for others less fortunate than they. Children can make presents; not buy them. A child can give his time, talents, and effort within the gift coupons he designs and gives to family members, friends, and special neighbors. Have your child decorate a plain card or piece of colored paper and write at the top: "A Gift For You From _____. At your request, I will . . . make a dress for your doll, bake your favorite dessert, baby-sit, weed your garden, clean your room, etc. These gift coupons can go into boxes and be wrapped like any other present.

Sadly, there are people who cannot give or receive without first checking the price tag or analyzing "what's in it for me?" These are often the same people who equate the amount spent on a gift with the amount of love or attention the gift conveys. Dan is twenty-nine, the only son of a widowed mother who lives several states away from his. He sends flowers on her birthday, remembers Mother's Day and Easter, and sends more gifts at Christmas. She phones each time to say "thank you and how much did you have to spend for that?" When she sends him a gift, she leaves the price tag on it because it is "easier to exchange" that way. Her motto is: "If you care as much as you should, you'll send only the most expensive."

Not all reasons for gift giving are positive

I have even known people (only a few, fortunately) who buy a present at a chain store and then shift it to a box from an expensive boutique. In their minds it isn't the gift that counts, it's the box that matters. While I assume these are extreme examples, and from only a minority of the population, they do remind us that the motivation for giving is not always admirable. As we set the positive patterns of generosity for our children, we are aware there is a negative counterpart which I call, gullibility. Yes, we want our children to give to others — but do we want them to give away everything they own? Are they selfish when they don't give an expensive new toy to a friend? Are we proud or worried if our children appear to let others "talk them out of everything"? Generosity is the impetus for healthy giving, but giving to compensate for a lack of self-esteem, buy a friendship, build self-confidence — these are negative forces for giving, and we must help our children discriminate between the right and the wrong reasons to give. The children in the following examples obviously are motivated by sincerity and the best intentions.

One child told me about the Christmas party she gives to her friends every year. "We spread an old bed sheet on the dining room table and in the center I put boxes of trimmings — bits of felt, cotton, sparkles, stars, ribbons, gold foil, and pieces of shiny material. My friends each have a few Styrofoam balls and a small tube of liquid glue. My mom puts on Christmas records and sometimes we sing carols while we make our ornaments. I serve punch and fancy cookies and my friends take home their ornaments and an extra plate of cookies for their families."

Another child described how his family "adopted" a child from a Third World nation as part of their giving to each other. "We all contributed money from our allowances and our jobs, and we sent our donation to an agency that sponsors poor children. We got a picture of our "adopted" child and a couple of times we even got letters from him. It's neat. We add to our fund all year and at Christmastime we send a special package of food and toys." When children discover the rewards — and the fun — of giving their time, talents, and energy, the glitter of a shopping mall dulls by comparison. Moreover, they are learning the patterns of another form of giving: volunteerism.

Volunteering: another form of giving

There are many ways children can volunteer their abilities. Libraries have programs where older people tutor younger ones. Hospitals and senior citizen centers welcome contributions of children who perform various tasks and provide entertainment. Churches and synagogues have endless needs for the talents and time of young people. Some work in the gardens of the property, some help with painting projects, supervise in the nurseries during a service, serve meals, or raise money through sales of baked goods, crafts, and car washes. In an election year, political campaign headquarters clutch at any hands that can fold, stuff, seal, or file.

Encourage your children to volunteer in less structured ways. For example, Bob picked up the morning paper and left it at a neighbor's door when he learned she was just home from the hospital. Betty took care of a neighbor's cat when the family had to visit a sick relative. Jack and Martha took homemade cookies and flowers to a new neighbor. Dick spent an hour after school reading to a younger child who was recovering from eye surgery. All these act of kindness, help, thoughtfulness, as well as all forms of charity, are the very patterns that perpetuate our American tradition of giving.

Teaching your child concern for the less fortunate

Not long ago, the *Wall Street Journal* published an article on their editorial page titled, "Will The Young Give As Well As They Get?" The author expressed his concern that an all-encompassing pursuit of boundless acquisitiveness would leave no time or energy for service organizations, nonprofit institutions, or personal contributions to our society. He wrote: "Time [is] even more valuable than money because it can't be replaced or replenished." One question this writer raised is the very question we answer when we teach our children how to give. "Can young people who have never known anything but good times feel strongly about others less fortunate?" Clearly, I believe they can and they will — if we show them how while they are growing up.

Appreciating the good that comes from payment of taxes

There is one way in which we all give and usually with a negative emotion. I refer to our taxes. We receive a salary, pension, allowance — some form of income. Every time we spend our money we also give additional funds, in the form of a tax, to pave our streets, pay for services from the police and fire departments, have a library, and give our children their schools! Obviously, I have listed only a sample of the many goods and services we receive when we give our taxes. But children should know that when they buy a five-dollar gift and actually pay five dollars and thirty cents for it, they are also giving to their community. Too often this form of giving and receiving is left out of a child's financial education. Perhaps if he knows he contributes to his community, he will have a higher regard for all he receives in return. Even adults forget the cause and effect relationship between their taxes and their environment. When I see anyone, child or adult, litter the park where he just enjoyed a picnic lunch, I think to myself, "Hey, you paid a tax when you bought that paper bag so you could have a clean park in which to eat your lunch. Then you throw your paper on the ground, someone is paid to clean it up, and maybe next time you buy a sandwich bag your tax will be higher. Have you ever wondered why?" I would like to suggest that once in a while when you go for a walk with your children, or drive them to the library, a park, or to school, point out all the goods and services your family receives in return for giving taxes to local, state, and federal governments. This will not make it fun to pay taxes, but it increases your child's awareness of this abstract process in which we all participate.

Sometimes volunteer work is bread cast upon the waters

On an equally pragmatic note, I'd like to make an additional remark about volunteering. Certainly children receive inner benefits when they donate their time and talents to community organizations and institutions. But there is a strong possibility (a probability!) they will someday receive an external reward as well. Let me tell you a true story (I'll change the name but that's all).

One summer when Ann was in junior high, she volunteered to work in the office of a nonprofit organization. She worked there five days a week, from nine to five, and did not earn one cent. Her job wasn't very exciting: she answered the phone, collected and opened the mail, stuffed envelopes, cleaned the shelves in a storeroom — all those dramatic adventures in the life of a small office. She may not have had a position of authority, she may not have been the one to decide policy and action, but she was an attentive observer and an alert listener. Years later, when Ann graduated from college, the director of that nonprofit organization wrote a letter of recommendation for her that led to an advantageous first step in her career. Furthermore, many of the skills Ann learned in that volunteer job prepared her for a position with considerably more responsibility than she otherwise would have had.

Your child's sense of generous giving as a volunteer is not diminished when you explain, with a proper perspective, the many rewards a volunteer receives. On the contrary, a complete and honest appraisal of why and how we donate to others prevents us from assuming the unattractive posture of a do-gooder.

It's not <u>always</u> better to give than to receive

We all are familiar with the refrain, "It is better to give than to receive." I understand the intent of the phrase, but I'm not sure I totally agree with it. There are too many times when the kindest and most generous act is to receive and let another have the joy of giving. There is no one-way street for any gift of any description — there is always a circle pattern when we give and receive.

As a final illustration of this pattern, let me describe a gift my own child received when she was eight years old and used as a way to give to others during all the years until she graduated from high school. The gift is called a "What-Not Box." A "What-Not Box" is a gift any child can use as soon as he or she is old enough to handle sharp objects like scissors or messy products like glue. Find a very sturdy box about the size of a suit box. Cover the lid, both the top and the sides, with solid-colored wrapping paper. Gold or silver is particularly attractive for this. Use rickrack or narrow ribbon that will adhere with liquid glue to form a frame on the top of the box about two inches in from each edge. Cut out letters from paper of a contrasting color, and within the frame (in the upper portion) add the child's name followed by the box description: "David's What-Not Box." Under the cut out letters, past or glue a greeting card as an additional decoration.

Put any of the following items in the box: tracing paper, paper doilies, crayons, pastels, drawing pencils, an artist's tablet, colored sheets of paper, foil paper, pipe cleaners, a hole punch, scissors, glue, transparent tape, cotton balls, assorted scraps of fabric and ribbons, packages of stickers, envelopes, a pencil sharpener, ruler, yarn, felt scraps, colored pencils, gold and silver stars, tubes of various colors of glitter, an art eraser, an outline form (for circles, triangles, and other shapes), an assorted collection of pictures cut from the front portion of your used greeting cards, and perhaps a small book of ideas for gifts you can make.

This is not an inexpensive gift! The contents add up to a considerable investment. But the investment lasts at least ten years, it produces extraordinary returns for a child, and it stimulates his creativity with ways he can give to others.

I never realized it before (in fact, not until this very moment while describing a "What-Not Box" for you), but this is the exact opposite of that well-known box belonging to Pandora. As you recall, according to the Greek myth she opened her box and exposed the world to all its misfortunes. It is gratifying to know that by exposing our children to our beliefs in the art of giving and the grace of receiving, they are prepared to counter misfortunes with their generosity.

9.
Equal But Separate

Some like it hot; some like it cold. Put two adults with different preferences under one roof where each has a hand on the thermostat, and there is bound to be considerable juggling to control the temperature. A change in either direction, higher or lower, makes the domestic environment uncomfortable for one or the other who shares it. Put a spender and a saver together under one roof and their domestic scene is a disaster unless they can moderate their differences.

When two parents with distinct ideas about money share the mutual responsibility for their child's financial education, a compromise is essential or the child receives inconsistent signals. Her environment is pandemonium! Imagine a child's reaction when her father says, "Don't forget the fair opens next week. You'd better save your allowance if you want money for the rides." Then, a few days later, her mother says, "You'll need money for the fair. Here — will ten dollars be enough?"

A child needs consistent training from both parents

These parents need to talk. Not only is one parent undermining the efforts of the other in teaching their child to manage money, but the discord between them can destroy their marriage. (Unresolved financial disputes are the second leading cause for divorce in America.) Perhaps the parents should list their ideas about money, identify and compare the differences, and discuss how they can reach a compromise. Both parents may have to suffer a little discomfort or their child will suffer a lot.

When parents do divorce and live under separate roofs, they

have an even greater challenge in giving their child equal money messages. Unfortunately, many divorced parents use their child as a weapon or as convenient leverage to manipulate the former spouse. According to government statistics, most children of divorced parents continue to live with their mother, and visit their father on a part-time basis. Reports indicate that following divorce the income of most women decreases, while for most men, it increases. These changes cause anger and resentment, fueling retaliation and competition between the parents for their child's allegiance. Add stepparents (and perhaps, stepchildren), and family finances are flung in so many directions it becomes an awesome task to juggle allowances, privileges, and responsibilities so that each child is treated fairly and all children are treated equally. I'm sure you know of situations similar to those I discovered when these divorced parents told me their dilemmas.

Bill has remarried. He and his new wife, Jane, live with her two girls from a former marriage. His first wife, Alice, and their three children live some distance away. When his children come to visit, there is a great deal of tension in the combined family. Alice distributes money to her three children using the "handout" method and does not expect them to do any chores at home. Bill and Jane give her two girls weekly allowances and require them to perform a number of household tasks. To compound the tension, Alice's parents live near their former son-in-law; when their grandchildren visit their father, this is the time the grandparents entertain the three youngsters with outings to amusement parks, baseball games, and movies. Jane's two daughters stay home. It's hard enough to unscramble the relationships; the big hurdle is finding solutions. What would you do to make the solution fair and equal?

The first step I would take is to have Bill tell his former wife he will provide their children with spending money while they visit him. He should also plan some special activities for his stepdaughters when his own children are being entertained by grandparents. All the children should be excused from chores during the visit, or else the chores should be shared by the five youngsters. These solutions are not perfect, but they provide some equality in an imperfect situation.

A less complicated example of the problems for divorced

parents is the case of Art and Sue. Their two children live with their mother and visit Art on weekends. His job necessitates frequent travel, often without much advance notice, so in spite of the arrangement, his children rarely see him. Art told me, "Last week I went through my check stubs to see where my money is going. I'm successful, but I have little to show for it. I discovered I spend most of my money on my kids, that's as it should be. I haven't been able to spend much time with them, but I make up for it every way I can."

Sue gave me her views. "I might as well toss allowances out the window for all the good they do my children. Art came back from one of his business trips and brought the kids the same records I've been telling them they had to save for and buy with their own money." These parents must discuss their common interest, their children, and find a way to work together for the benefit of their offspring. Art cannot use gifts or money as substitutes for time with his children. Sue needs to let Art know how she is teaching the children to manage money. Communication could ease the friction if both parents are willing to cooperate.

Shouldn't the well-being of the children come first?

But as we know, a list of the top ten reasons for divorce has yet to include good communication or splendid cooperation. Not all parents are willing to work together; they prefer to concentrate on their own feelings, and often their children become pawns in games of one-upsmanship. "Mom, look at this radio Dad gave me. Boy, he's neat!" This child will receive a portable television just as soon as Mom can get to a store. "Dad, see the skates Mom bought me. She sure is super!" Here's a child who will receive a bicycle when Dad goes shopping on the weekend. If one of these parents will listen to reason, he or she will realize that the only way to end this game is to refuse to play. This is not an easy solution. But a parent who truly cares about the well-being of the children will be willing to accept some painful consequences.

And what if the parents will not listen to reason? Then it won't take long before their child figures out that one-upsmanship is her best game in town. Using her parents as pawns, she deliberately maneuvers them into competitive situations to serve her interests. When this happens, parents receive painfully expensive consequences, and their child acquires detrimental, manipulative behavior techniques.

I know it is difficult for parents to present a united front when dealing with their children. Spontaneous events occur, and in even the best of situations, one parent will deal with it one way while the other will take a different approach. Despite our knowing that the best decisions are reached after discussing the choices involved, what happens when one parent cannot get cooperation from the other? True, this happens more often when the parents are divorced, but it also occurs when one parent is preoccupied, travels frequently, or simply chooses not to be involved. Under these circumstances, one parent must assume the full responsibility for giving his or her children the best possible financial education.

Children are perceptive; fortunately, they are also resilient. They may not show now that they recognize a parent who is willing to forfeit his or her own satisfaction in order to provide the most favorable conditions for them, but life can be fair. They *do* recognize it and they will acknowledge it when they are older.

10.
Purse
Strings

You may think my crystal ball is cracked when I forecast a conclusion to this financial education you are giving your children. Their graduation from dependency to autonomy is particularly hard to envision while you stand in a bedroom doorway marveling that anyone can survive the confusion of stuffed animals, homework, toys, games, clothes, sports equipment, and shriveled apple cores.

However, your children will not only survive the chaos of growing up; thanks to you, they will walk away from it carrying a complete package of financial skills with which to craft a successful future.

They have confidence in their ability to earn money.

They are judicious in how they spend money.

They save it. They share their resources with others.

They are familiar with basic investment opportunities.

They have healthy attitudes toward money meshed with realistic regard for its value.

They are well-equipped to meet the challenges in their adult financial circumstances.

They have been taught responsible behavior; let them apply those lessons

It is ironic, but it is at this threshold to the future when many parents undermine the very purpose of the financial education they provided. Now that their children have it, the parents won't let them use it. More often than not, the motivation for parents who are reluctant to allow their adult children financial freedom comes from the best of intentions, including generosity, devotion, and love. Frequently these best intentions lead to unfortunate results not too different from those motivated by self-serving interests.

Lisa has been working for three years and earns a good salary. Her money-management skills enable her to rent a nice apartment, entertain her friends, and enjoy many of the pleasures in life. Twice a year her parents come for a brief visit and never during their stay do they allow her to pay for anything. Dad has his credit cards out before the gas tank is full, the waiter brings the check, or the box office opens. Mom has her wallet out as the checker rings up the grocery total, the salesperson folds the sweater, or the paperboy rings the doorbell. "When my folks come to visit," says Lisa, "they refuse to act like guests. They make it look as if I can't afford to take care of myself, let alone entertain them. I'm used to being independent and my parents raised me to believe self-sufficiency is an important goal for every adult. When they grab the check it makes me feel I have failed their expectations — that I'm a little girl again with an allowance from my parents. It's degrading!"

Lisa's parents see their actions in a different light. "We're so proud of our daughter — she is most capable, and we admire her independence. We know it isn't easy for her to manage on what she earns, so when we go for a visit we want to do everything we can to be a help and not a burden." Her mother adds, "I remember when I was starting out in life and relatives would come to visit expecting me to buy all the extra food plus show them a good time. I learned a lesson from that and I swore I'd never impose on my children when they were grown up."

Time to let go; she's an adult now (thanks to you!)

It is wrenching to break the pattern of helping our offspring but there are times when we must curtail our generous good habits so our children are released to function as liberated adults. Sadly, there are parents who don't want to liberate their adult children.

Sally's father sat in the living room one evening telling his guests about his daughter's success. After his recital of her impressive new job, he remarked, "Oh, that daughter of mine. Her American Express statement arrived today and you wouldn't believe her list of charges. Her bills read like a map: New York for the theater, Bermuda for a vacation, back to Los Angeles. From the names of the restaurants and the shops at least I know I don't have to worry she's starving to death or doesn't have a thing to wear."

I probably should have kept my mouth shut, but I was so amazed by his obvious boast masked as a complaint that I blurted out, "Do you mean your daughter still uses your charge cards?"

"Oh, I'm sure she wants to be independent," he said, "but this is her way of staying in touch with the family. I think it's kind of sweet she wants her dad to know she is still his little girl."

Balderdash! (I didn't say it, but I thought it.) This young woman is no more independent than when she was in the third grade and daddy bought her an ice cream cone. I suspect, too, that the father is the one who wants his daughter to remain his little girl and he is willing to pay the price to keep her dependent upon him.

"Greenmail" — a disservice to your adult child

Purse strings, even when held in generous and loving hands, have a way of pulling and tugging against the emotional needs of adult children to feel competent, self-reliant, proud, and autonomous. And some parents, like Sally's father, use purse strings as apron strings. Money is the bind that ties. Maybe someday it will strangle and destroy the family relationship.

The telephone is the most convenient instrument parents can use to keep their adult children within the sound of mommy's and daddy's voice. Despite frequent complaints by parents about the horrendous size of their long distance phone bills, they would rather pay the cost than cut the cord. Typically these parents say: "We know our kids can't afford big long distance bills, but we want them to feel free to call us at least once a week so they can stay in touch." It doesn't occur to them that Sue, Dick, or Harry might resent staying in touch each week but they have little choice when "free" communication is applied as leverage to keep them connected to their parents.

When parents offer financial assistance to their adult children, regardless of the motivation, there can be an emotional cost involved in the gift or the loan. Parents must be extremely sensitive to this subtle surcharge which I label "emotional greenmail." "Dear, your father and I want to give you a car. Won't it be nice for you to have your own transportation? Now you can drive over to visit us all the time." Or, "Son, guess what? We're sending you a check for airplane tickets so you can come home for your birthday — and Christmas, and your vacation, and..." These illustrations of helping hands — the credit cards, collect phone calls, cars, tickets — come from parents who sincerely want to give support to their children but fail to see their help includes a surcharge. Not all help, however, is offered with unintentional emotional greenmail attached to the gesture.

Shocking as it is, I hear parents admit: "We make a point of helping our children now because someday they may have to help us; we want to be sure they know they owe a debt to their parents." In my opinion, any parent who tries to manipulate his or her children with financial leverage for the present or the future deserves to receive negative repercussions.

Self-respect that has been earned must be respected

One young woman I know who graduated with honors from her parents' course in financial education recognized a potential unpleasantness. After several years in the work force, Nancy decided to return to school and study for her doctorate. Her parents were more than able to give her full financial support while she attended graduate school; they gladly offered her tuition, room and board, transportation, and a generous living allowance. She explained her decision by saying, "I decided to attend _____ university because they gave me a full scholarship and a teaching fellowship that will let me be self-supporting. Another university had a lot more status and prestige, but going there would have meant I'd have to borrow from my family. This way I can continue to be independent and not feel beholden to my parents in any way. I know they want the best for me and I appreciate their generosity, but they taught me the satisfaction of being self-reliant. If I change the situation now, I'm not sure what it might do to our relationship. The reputation of a graduate school is less important to me than my self-respect and the harmony I have with my parents."

In many families there is this sense of harmony and mutual respect: a willingness to offer help, a freedom to accept or refuse it, and a clear understanding between the generations that money or material assistance transfers without an emotional cost. For some families, in fact, helping each other to the extent of their ability is a tradition, and the thought of purse strings seems absurd and irrelevant. Perhaps you will find the same pleasure I did when I learned about some of these traditions. They include: a car, furniture, shares of stock, handmade quilts, a freezer full of meat and homegrown vegetables, an assortment of "mom's" jams and jellies, family recipes, a supply of garden tools — in one family, the tradition of a down-payment for a first house is now in the fourth generation! Many adult children recognize their parents' need to feel useful and that often the only way this can be expressed is through giving money or material goods. It requires sensitivity from both generations if economic resources are to be passed along without an erosion of the family relationships.

The gift of financial literacy can endure

Whether or not you received financial assistance when you left home, as the parents of a new generation you have the opportunity to form your own traditions for helping your children achieve future success. There is no greater gift you can transmit to your children than the financial education you provide. To illustrate, imagine a child receives a great library but has not learned to read. In effect, he receives nothing of value. When, however, he learns how to read, then there is not one word inaccessible to him and not one word he cannot use to his advantage.

When you give the gift of financial literacy to your children, they receive a legacy of enduring value, one with a wealth unequaled in dollars. Moreover, a legacy of information about money cannot be adversely affected by economic conditions. It remains intact, with the potential to grow, as it passes from one generation to the next and to the next.

Index